THE MOTIVATIONAL MIND:

EMPOWERING YOUR MINDSET FOR GREATNESS

BY BEN BANDER

TABLE OF CONTENTS

INTRODUCTION 1

UNDERSTANDING THE POWER OF POSITIVITY 4

MIND YOUR MIND, YOU ARE WHAT YOU THINK 12

THE POWER OF A POSITIVE MINDSET 20

SIMPLIFIED METHODS TO ESTABLISH AND SUSTAIN POSITIVE THINKING 25

HOW CAN YOU ASSIST IN IMPROVING YOUR MOOD? 35

RECOGNIZING ADVERSE PATTERNS AND THE PRACTICAL IMPLICATIONS OF NEGATIVE INDIVIDUALS AND ENVIRONMENTS 44

SIMPLIFIED METHODS FOR CONFRONTING NEGATIVE THOUGHTS 56

HOW TO DOMINATE OVER NEGATIVE THOUGHTS 65

USE POSITIVE THOUGHTS TO BRING YOUR DREAMS TO LIFE 72

BREAKING FREE FROM NEGATIVITY AND CHALLENGING LIMITING BELIEFS 76

WHAT IS RESTRICTING YOUR PROGRESS? 88

STRATEGIES FOR CONQUERING NEGATIVE SELF-TALK 97

MANAGING REJECTION AND CRITICISM 105

EMBRACE AFFIRMATIONS OF SELF-CONFIDENCE 114

STRATEGIES AND METHODS FOR ENHANCING SELF-ESTEEM 118

UNDERSTANDING THE POWER OF OPTIMISM 125

NAVIGATING TOXIC RELATIONSHIPS AND NEGATIVE INDIVIDUALS 135

DO YOU PRIORITIZE THE NEGATIVE COMMENTS OF YOUR PEERS OR YOUR DREAMS? 146

DEVELOP A SPIRITUAL AND POSITIVE LIFESTYLE WITHOUT EVEN RUNNING AWAY FROM YOUR COMFORT ZONE 152

REALIZE YOUR ASPIRATIONS THROUGH POSITIVE THINKING ... 160

BEN'S MOTIVATIONAL QUOTES 165

CONCLUSION 168

AUTHOR BIO 170

INTRODUCTION

Amidst the fast-paced environment of our everyday existence, rife with difficulties and susceptibility to negativity, an extraordinary force lurks the power of positivity.

This book digs deep into the human mind to uncover techniques that can help us stay optimistic, even when life gets tough.

Life throws a lot of curveballs that can test our ability to remain positive. This book is like a guiding light, aiming to lead readers to a more upbeat and fulfilling life.

Using the latest research in psychology, neuroscience and personal growth, "The

As you turn these pages, you'll go on a transformative journey. You'll learn where pessimism comes from, gain skills to overcome self-doubt, and cultivate new resources to maintain an uplifting mindset.

You will gain an understanding of the complexities of human relationships, including the consequences of negative influences and how to establish a positive, supportive social network.

To foster personal development, improving interpersonal connections or attaining career advancement, this book provides readers with the fundamental mindset and strategies necessary to effectuate significant life changes.

Being positive goes way beyond just being optimistic. Having a sunny outlook can actually spark creativity, help you make better choices, and make you more resilient when times get rough. When you adopt a positive mindset, you open yourself up to a world of opportunities, healthy relationships, and success.

Letter from the Author

Dear Reader,

As you turn the pages of this book, I hope you find more than just words; I hope you discover a journey towards understanding, kindness, and self-love. It's essential to remember that no one will love and understand you in the profound ways you can love and understand yourself. In the pursuit of happiness and fulfillment, adopting a positive mindset is crucial. It allows us to see beyond the immediate hurdles and embrace a future filled with possibilities.

Life is an intricate tapestry of experiences, some uplifting and others challenging.

It's vital to acknowledge that while we cannot change our past, we possess the power to craft our future. This belief is not just about ambition or goals; it's about the fundamental choice to surround ourselves with positivity and to move away from negativity that weighs us down. Toxic relationships, those that drain rather than enrich your spirit, deserve no place in your life. If you've done your part in trying to mend what's broken and it still doesn't work, know that it's okay to move on. Your effort was not in vain; it was a step towards understanding what you truly deserve.

In this journey of life, remember the principle of karma: "Do good, and good will come to you." Sharing your knowledge, your care, and your kindness without expecting anything in return not only enriches those around you but also brings an inner peace and satisfaction that material rewards cannot match. It's about creating a ripple of positivity that, in time, can turn into a wave of change for the better.

In your professional and personal life, you may encounter jealousy and negativity, perhaps from colleagues or even a manager. Such experiences, while disheartening, are not reflections of your worth but rather reflections of their limitations.

Never let their skepticism or sarcasm about your achievements undermine your confidence. Remember, their inability to see your value does not decrease your worth.

Be confident, be strong, and always look forward. Just as birds soar higher and the clouds part to accommodate their flight, let your spirit and ambitions fly high. The challenges you face, much like the clouds, are not barriers but opportunities to rise above and reach new heights.

In closing, I invite you to carry these thoughts with you as you navigate through life's complexities. Let kindness be your compass and positivity your path. Believe in yourself, in the beauty of your dreams, and in the power you hold to shape your destiny. Remember, every moment is a chance to write a new chapter, to craft a future filled with joy, fulfillment, and love.

Ben Bander Abudawood

10/11/2023

UNDERSTANDING THE POWER OF POSITIVITY

A positive demeanor is an optimistic outlook on life. A person with a positive attitude is certain that favorable outcomes will transpire and is confident in their ability to influence such events.

The glass is half filled in their estimation, not half empty. They maintain an optimistic outlook rather than fixating on the negative.

Positive thinking offers many advantages. It can assist you in maintaining your mental and physical health.

Positive-thinking individuals are at a reduced risk of developing depression and anxiety. Furthermore, they are more likely to enjoy satisfying relationships and achieve professional success.

Positive thinking can also assist one in managing tension and adversity. A positive outlook has the potential to provide the fortitude necessary to overcome obstacles. Also, it can assist you in overcoming obstacles and sustaining your motivation.

Many actions can be taken to enhance one's perspective on life. Spend time with optimistic individuals, read motivational narratives and look for daily opportunities to chuckle. Motivate yourself to transform your aspirations into tangible accomplishments by imagining yourself in that position. Always remember that a positive outlook can complete the transformation.

Supposedly, having a positive attitude is the key to success in life, according to The Law of Attraction. But being positive offers lots of other benefits too.

When you start each day with an optimistic outlook, you're more likely to see the good in situations and people. It also becomes easier to stay motivated and focused on your goals. Plus, positivity can help reduce stress and anxiety.

You can build a positive mindset by keeping a cheerful attitude, even when things get difficult. It's also important to have a strong support system of upbeat people to help keep you motivated. Remember to celebrate your wins, even small ones. And try not to dwell on negative thoughts or experiences.

The following are a few suggestions for cultivating a positive attitude:

- Every day, make an effort to identify things for which you are thankful and set aside time to reflect on the positive aspects of your existence.

-It is a personal challenge always to find the silver lining in any circumstance, regardless of its difficulty.

-Bless others more often, offer compliments, participate in spontaneous acts of kindness or otherwise endeavor to disseminate positivity.

- Concentrate on your unique qualities and personal strengths; - Commemorate your accomplishments, no matter how minor.

-Consider all the reasons why you are deserving of happiness and success by creating a positive affirmation list or board!

Having a positive attitude is seen as really important for achieving success. Though people define it differently, a positive attitude basically means having an optimistic view of life and believing good things will happen.

Those with a sunny outlook tend to be more successful and happy overall. They also attract others to them and bounce back better when faced with challenges.

So cultivating positivity is a great first step if you want to make even small improvements in your life. Here are some of the main benefits of having a positive attitude:

1. You will experience greater happiness.

A positive outlook on life tends to result in an inherent state of happiness. This is because you focus on positive developments instead of fixating on negative ones. Adopting the half full rather than half empty perspective can cultivate an atmosphere of optimism and positivity regarding the future.

2. You Will Obtain Greater Success

Individuals with a positive attitude consistently have a greater chance of success in all they undertake.

This is due to their self-confidence and conviction in their capacity to accomplish their goals. They are unfazed by setbacks and disappointments and instead use them as inspiration to persevere.

3. Enhancing Your Attractiveness to Others

Possessing a positive attitude causes one to emanate enticing positive energies toward others. Friends and potential companions are more likely to be attracted to you if you emanate happiness and optimism since people are naturally drawn to those who make them feel good.

4. You will develop enhanced resilience in the face of adversity.

It's impossible to live a perfect life - everyone faces hardship at some point.

But you'll be better at dealing with adversity if you keep a positive attitude.

This is because you can maintain an optimistic view and find the silver lining in any situation, staying hopeful that things will get better in the end.

5. You will attain a longer lifespan.

Research shows pessimists tend to have shorter lifespans than optimists.

This is likely because they deal with less anxiety and stress, which can negatively impact health over time. So developing a positive mindset is key to living a long, healthy life.

Building a positive attitude is never easy, but it's always worthwhile.

You'll achieve more success and happiness, and be better able to handle whatever life throws your way. So start giving thanks, focusing on the good in your life, and letting go of negative thoughts and feelings. You'll notice a shift in your overall outlook.

Having a positive disposition creates positive energy. It's believing positive outcomes are possible and you can make them happen. An optimistic view empowers you to make determined choices, opening up lots of chances for success.

A positive attitude also attracts positive experiences and people into your life. In essence, positive energy brings about good outcomes.

A positive outlook can aid in overcoming challenging circumstances and developing resilience in the face of adversity.

Therefore, to experience the manifold advantages of maintaining a positive attitude, you must first develop a more optimistic perspective on existence. Engage in enjoyable activities, surround yourself with positive people and reflect daily on what you are grateful for. You can change your attitude for the best and enjoy all the benefits that accompany it with minimal effort.

Beginning with one's mindset, a positive attitude can significantly influence one's existence. Start your journey toward enhancing your perspective on life by consciously committing to thinking more positively. You will be amazed at how much better you feel and how much more enjoyable your life becomes when you concentrate on the positive.

Outcome of Negative Thinking

The main result of negative thinking is feeling more negative emotions and thoughts. This can lower your confidence instead of raising it up. Having a negative inner voice can hurt your self-assurance and stop you from reaching your full potential.

Lack of sleep, cold symptoms, fatigue, stress, and hunger can all trigger negative self-talk. Spending too much time alone with negative thoughts can lead to depression.

Psychologists have also found negative thinking contributes to OCD, constant worry, anxiety and depression. This negativity also greatly affects the brain. Research shows negative thinking may increase the risk of dementia.

One form of negative thinking is emotional reasoning. This is when you believe something is true just because of how you feel. For example, feeling lonely and thinking "No one wants to be around me because I'm so lonely."

Another is mind reading - when you make assumptions about what others think of you, usually negatively.

How Can I Cease Negative Thought Processes?

What measures can be implemented to cease or prevent the occurrence of these negative, purposeless thoughts?

To cultivate positive emotions instead of negative ones, one must develop an awareness of their emotions. It has been established that there are circumstances in which the approach of a black hole can't be detected.

It is advisable to pause before forming an opinion, expressing it, or passing judgment on any notion. Doing so would prompt one to consider whether such actions induce feelings of depression, negativity or melancholy. You must be capable of controlling these emotions if they are genuinely yours; otherwise, they should not be detrimental to you.

Listed below are some techniques for enhancing your disposition:

In the end, they are merely "thoughts." It doesn't make them true: It is essential to remember that visualizing certain fearful events doesn't automatically guarantee their actualization.

The purpose of pondering is to provide visual gratification so one can form personal opinions by utilizing one's human potential. Self-praising is the most effective course of action. Compensating for the negativity generated internally is akin to excavating one's tomb.

Be mindful of your current emotions:

Experiencing any sorrow you may manifest. However, resist the temptation to delude that this is your permanent state of mind. You can prevent these awful emotions from becoming your reality by resisting the urge to be consumed by them.

Create a positive environment by appreciating the joy in the smallest details. Also, you may encounter something humorous.

Have a night of complete slumber.

Practice judicious eating. Enhancing one's physical well-being is directly correlated with engaging in physical activity.

Appreciate your benefits; every one of us has a great deal for which to be thankful. What do you hold in high regard?

Developing your social skills is, in essence, an extension of the adage "create the neighborhood you desire." Make an effort to spend quality time with your family, colleagues and other cherished individuals. Select the religion that fulfills your needs the most. Join a group or crew. Start investigating a new hobby.

When you comprehend negative affectivity, negative notions will become irrelevant. In addition, therapy for negative thought disorders enables the patient to concentrate on regulating negative emotions and finding happiness in the smallest pleasures.

MIND YOUR MIND, YOU ARE WHAT YOU THINK

Even though the human mind is widely acknowledged to be quite potent, very few individuals are mindful of its strength. It is widely held that an individual lacks control over their thoughts.

Even passing thoughts can temporarily bring down your self-esteem. It's normal for it to go up and down a bit. But problems happen when those thoughts start to shape how you see yourself.

Self-esteem is so important to who we are. By getting rid of negative beliefs and growing more positive ones, you can build a healthy mindset and positive self-image.

What factors contribute to low self-esteem?

The reasons for low self-esteem often come from early life experiences. Key moments while growing up play a big role in shaping someone's self-esteem and personality down the road.

Kids tend to take on the mindset and behavior of people who influenced them a lot during their development.

Those behaviors shape their thinking, reasoning, and self-image.

So people who consistently saw negative patterns are more likely to have negative beliefs about themselves, leading to low self-worth.

But stressful life events that have already happened can also contribute to low self-esteem - like losing a loved one, business failures, breakups, money troubles, or mistreatment from a parent, partner, sibling, or caregiver.

While low self-esteem has the potential to influence nearly all facets of an individual's existence, its detrimental effects on mental health can be overpowering. Individuals who suffer from reduced self-esteem may confront the subsequent obstacles:

Relationship impairment:
A low sense of self-worth is often accompanied by negative emotions and a low view of one's worth, which profoundly impacts interpersonal interactions. It can harm one's mental health and tranquility by introducing additional contradictions and conflicts into relationships.

Vulnerability to addiction:
People with low self-esteem often turn to drugs, alcohol or other substances as a way to escape their pain. But over time, these coping methods can lead to full-blown addiction, which can have disastrous results.

Depression:

Low self-esteem can cause feelings of helplessness and worry, pushing emotions in a negative direction. It takes a psychological toll by promoting sadness and causing anxiety.

Nevertheless, by implementing specific self-help strategies, it is possible to repel adverse emotions and cultivate a sense of optimism and general welfare.

The following are methods for managing negative thinking:

- Cognitive Restructuring: Identify negative thoughts, evaluate them objectively, and reframe them in a more positive light. For example, countering "I always mess up" with "I have succeeded many times in the past."

- Mindfulness: Practice staying rooted in the present moment to detach from negative thoughts. Meditation and breathing exercises can help you refocus on the here and now when negativity strikes.

- Positive Self-Talk: Counteract negative inner voices by cultivating an encouraging inner dialogue with positive affirmations. Repeat phrases like "I am strong enough to handle this."

- Gratitude Journaling: Write down things you are grateful for every day to foster appreciation rather than negative feelings. Focus on little joys and accomplishments.

- Limit Negative Influences: Cut back news consumption if it fuels negativity. Be picky about who and what you surround yourself with.

- Visualization: Picture yourself handling a situation skillfully. Imagining success can breed confidence.

- Being self-compassionate: An individual deserves the same or possibly greater empathy they would extend to others. Life is full of unavoidable mistakes and setbacks and cultivating self-compassion is fundamental to enhancing one's self-esteem.

Methods to Develop a Positive Mindset

In today's negative world, people often forget the power of positive thinking and gratitude. We focus too much on the bad things in life. This stops us from seeing the good things. It makes us feel unhappy and dissatisfied more often.

We tend to think too much about negative events. But we don't pay enough attention to the positive things that happen. This reduces our ability to feel grateful. When we can't appreciate the good things around us, it's harder to feel happy or deal with problems.

Negative thinking also harms our physical health. The stress from constant negativity can cause real health issues in our bodies. Our minds and bodies are connected, so negative thoughts can make existing conditions worse.

When we think negatively all the time, it becomes a habit. This makes it even harder to have positive thoughts. The negativity spreads to other parts of our lives too. It might make us unable to trust people, even loyal friends.

The good news is that just as negative thinking can be learned, so can positive thinking. By consciously cultivating a positive mindset, we can condition our minds to focus on the good and approach challenges with a solution-oriented attitude.

While we cannot avoid encountering negativity in life, we can choose how we respond to it.

When we approach negativity with a positive mindset, we open ourselves up to finding solutions and overcoming obstacles. Conversely, approaching problems with a negative attitude only drains our time and energy, hindering our progress.

Remember , we are all bound to encounter negativity at some point. Therefore, train your mind to approach negativity positively; if you begin finding a solution with a positive attitude, you will certainly arrive at one; conversely, if you begin contemplating a problem in a negative light, your time and energy will be wasted.

Best Methods for Positive Thinking;

Smiling upon awakening:

When you wake up in the morning, welcome the new day with a cheerful smile. This shows you are thankful for the chance to continue your adventure of self-improvement and success. Making gratitude part of your morning routine helps start your day off with positivity. It puts you in a good frame of mind to influence all the thoughts, deeds and conversations you'll have over the next 16 hours. When you make the effort to appreciate each new sunrise, it focuses your energy on all the potential that lies ahead. Waking up grateful keeps you motivated to enrich yourself and make progress on meaningful goals throughout your precious waking hours. Simply by embracing an attitude of thankfulness when you open your eyes, you set the tone for productivity, personal growth and making the most of every moment.

Watch a comedy clip or read something funny and that will cheer up your day.

The Power of Meditation - Cultivating Inner Tranquility

Try meditation - it's an old technique that helps people think more positively and feel calmer.

To truly understand meditation, you have to practice it yourself. Follow tips from experienced teachers to guide you.

Meditation gives your mind a break from stress so you feel more peaceful. Set aside some quiet time each day to sit alone without noise or distractions. Bring your attention to the present moment and your breathing. This helps quiet rushing thoughts so you can relax.

In this peaceful space, negative thinking patterns and worries tend to fade away. With regular practice, meditation can improve every part of life - you'll feel less anxious, relationships may even get better. After meditating, you feel refreshed and focused to achieve your goals.

Nowadays many people use this ancient skill to boost their success and happiness. Making meditation a habit is time well spent to reduce negativity.

The Company We Keep - A Reflection of Our Minds

Spend time with positive people - their upbeat attitude can rub off on you. Being around optimists helps you see the world in a better light. This doesn't happen instantly, but you'll notice a change over time after regular contact with positive influences. Their contagious hope and good energy will slowly alter how you view things. Bit by bit, your outlook will get brighter too. Even on the hardest days, positive friends can make you feel stronger. You'll discover their habits of highlighting the good, keeping perspective, and envisioning success are contagious. Before you know it, you naturally start adopting those attitudes yourself. Though the path to positivity requires patience, by joining forces with encouraging people who share their light with others, you ensure you ultimately reach your destination.

The Influence of Gatherings - Shaping Our Future Paths

The gatherings we choose to attend play a pivotal role in shaping our future paths. As your elders have wisely advised, select your company with care, for the right circle of peers can propel you towards success and fulfillment. Surround yourself with individuals who encourage you to reach your full potential, who celebrate your triumphs, and offer support during times of adversity.

Escaping the Toxicity of Negativity

Don't waste time arguing with negative people. Debating those who only see the downside is pointless and draining. Seek out thoughtful discussions where ideas are exchanged respectfully and common ground is found.

People who are very negative tend to drag down others to feel better temporarily. Their words can stick with you and darken your whole day.

By keeping your distance from these individuals, you protect your positive mindset and mental health.

Instead, focus on positive thinking, gratitude, and supportive people who make you feel encouraged. This empowers you to live a fulfilling, joyful life.

By staying away from negative influences, you can stay focused on your goals with positivity. Save your energy for constructive conversations and people who inspire you to see the best in any situation. Limiting negativity helps you concentrate on the bright side.

THE POWER OF A POSITIVE MINDSET

Positive thinking can be defined as positive energy generated through positive self-talk or optimism in general but these are all still vague and general concepts.

To successfully cultivate positive thoughts and actions, utilizing tangible illustrations to aid in imaginative visualization is essential.

Let's proceed to deliberate on strategies for maintaining a positive attitude amidst this generally unfavorable situation:

Begin by speaking positively to yourself:

A positive mood can be established for the remainder of the day.

When you wake up late in the morning? You have begun to experience discomfort and continue to be in a rush to finish the day's duties.

This hassle can disrupt pondering and induce a negative frame of mind. Start your day with an optimistic mindset rather than succumbing to this frame of mind.

Engage in self-talk while standing in front of the mirror, even if it makes you feel foolish, by uttering affirmations such as "Today I will dedicate myself to improving my abilities" or "Today I will strive for excellence in my skill set." The transformation in your mindset will astound you.

Obtain joy from the smallest of things:

Almost certainly, one will encounter obstacles and mistakes at some point in their lifetime; no one lives without difficulties or flawlessly. Approach such an obstacle as a challenge and concentrate on the advantages of acquiring new knowledge today, regardless of how trivial it may appear. Try to extract the positive from each adversity you encounter.

For instance, when stuck in traffic, refrain from worrying about how late you are or anything similar; consider how you can use that time to listen to your favorite tracks.

Life is full of surprises, both pleasant and unexpected. When your favorite restaurant is closed or out of your favorite dish, instead of feeling disappointed, embrace the opportunity to try something new. Venture beyond your comfort zone and explore the vast array of culinary delights waiting to be discovered. View each new experience as an adventure, an opportunity to expand your horizons and cultivate a more adventurous spirit.

Positive thinking is a powerful tool that can transform your life. Incorporate positive affirmations into your daily routine, reminding yourself of your strengths, abilities, and dreams. Believe in yourself and your ability to achieve your goals. A positive mindset can open doors to new possibilities and help you overcome obstacles with greater resilience.

Challenge negative thoughts as they arise. Reframe them in a more positive light, focusing on the potential solutions rather than the problems. Remember that your perspective shapes your reality. By cultivating a positive outlook, you can attract more positive experiences into your life.

Positive energy is contagious. Surround yourself with people who inspire and uplift you, those who radiate positivity and encouragement. Their optimism will rub off on you, further fueling your own positive mindset.

Maintain an attitude of gratitude. Take time each day to appreciate the good things in your life, big and small. Expressing gratitude can shift your focus from what you lack to the abundance that already surrounds you.

Remember that you have the power to control your thoughts and emotions. Don't let negative influences or circumstances dictate your state of mind. Choose to be positive, and you will reap the rewards of a more joyful and fulfilling life.

Your beliefs about yourself and the world have a profound impact on your actions and experiences. Believe in your potential and your ability to achieve your dreams. A positive self-image will empower you to take inspired action and create the life you desire.

Embrace the journey of self-discovery and personal growth. Explore new ideas, challenge your limiting beliefs, and expand your knowledge. As you grow and evolve, you will attract more positive experiences and opportunities into your life.

Remember that positive energy attracts positive results. Cultivate a positive mindset, surround yourself with positivity, and express gratitude for the abundance in your life. By doing so, you will create a life filled with joy, fulfillment, and success.

Employ positive thinking to achieve your goals.

It is not uncommon for most individuals to have a negative outlook on life today; however, you can change that outlook. You should begin by maintaining a positive attitude and striving to achieve your destiny.

It is advisable to avoid negative individuals who are not hesitant to dump frigid water on your plans. You can accomplish your goals by maintaining a positive attitude and remaining committed to realizing your destiny.

Suggestions for maintaining a positive outlook and realizing one's potential.

To reshape your destiny, cultivate a positive mindset and channel your inner strength. Embark on this journey by distancing yourself from negative influences that drain your energy and dampen your spirits. Instead, surround yourself with supportive individuals who share your aspirations and motivate you to reach your full potential.

Dedicate a portion of each day to reflect on your goals, keeping them at the forefront of your mind. This mental rehearsal will reinforce your determination and fuel your passion for achieving your dreams.

Avoid wasting your precious time and energy on frivolous pursuits. Instead, focus on activities that align with your goals and personal growth. Utilize your time wisely, making the most of every opportunity to learn, grow, and advance towards your aspirations.

Visualize your success vividly, immersing yourself in the details of your accomplishments. Imagine the immense satisfaction of achieving your goals, experiencing the feeling of joy and fulfillment that accompanies these victories.

Set ambitious goals that challenge you to expand your horizons and break through self-imposed limitations. Embrace the positive energy that arises from these aspirations, allowing it to guide your actions and propel you towards your desired outcomes.

Remember that your destiny is not predetermined; it is shaped by your choices, actions, and mindset.

Embrace the power of positive energy, and you will unlock the remarkable potential that lies within you.

The journey may not always be smooth, but with perseverance and unwavering belief in yourself, you can achieve anything you set your mind to. Embrace the challenges, learn from setbacks, and continuously strive for self-improvement.

Embrace the power of positive energy, and you will set in motion a chain of events that will lead you towards a brighter, more fulfilling future. Believe in yourself, dream big, and take action with unwavering determination. Your destiny awaits, ready to be shaped by your positive energy and unwavering spirit.

SIMPLIFIED METHODS TO ESTABLISH AND SUSTAIN POSITIVE THINKING

Having a positive attitude pays off in every part of life. Research shows that optimistic people are more productive at work and more creative. Positivity also boosts confidence, which allows you to thrive in all areas.

When you feel confident, it's easier to make wise choices instead of hesitating. Fear can shut down productive thinking. Worrying what people think may stopper decision-making and trying new things. While you overthink, opportunities pass by.

Emotions like regret, jealousy and anxiety tied to fear also damage health and lifestyle.

Personal growth courses reinforce positive habits and reduce negative ones - aligning your thoughts, feelings and actions. This raises wellbeing and life satisfaction.

Your mindset shapes your experiences. Choosing positivity opens doors to amazing possibilities.

Some tips for developing an optimistic mindset are:

Establish goals.

The path to lasting success is paved with a clearly defined roadmap that incorporates both immediate and far-reaching goals. It helps to think of it as a journey stretching out before you towards a distant horizon.

Let's imagine an aspiring swimmer who harbors dreams of one day competing in an open water charity swim, yet can't currently stay afloat. While that ultimate objective seems daunting from the shoreline, the process of achieving it becomes far less intimidating when broken down into smaller, more manageable milestones.

Establishing medium-term goals serves as an ascending staircase towards higher aspirations. Maybe completing ten lengths of the community pool would be an appropriate medium-term goal to orient towards. It presents enough challenge to feel invested, yet remains within the realm of possibility - a crucial source of motivation.

To keep chipping away and building confidence, integrating very short-term goals into the master plan proves essential. The sense of accomplishment and belief in one's capabilities derived from achieving bite-sized targets, like half a length across the pool, creates the momentum needed to propel forward.

With each smaller goal reached, take time to actively reward efforts and revel in development. These self-celebrations, whether material treats or simple pats on the back, positively reinforce progress made. They refuel energy tanks to keep striving farther, even during periods where the final destination sits obscured behind clouds of uncertainty.

Ascending to success demands not a furious sprint but rather a determined marathon pace marked by restorations. With ample milestones mapped out along the path at digestible intervals, even the boldest dreams materialize if given the runway to become reality. The key is tailoring the steps so they entice rather than overwhelm.

Possess self-confidence.

Therefore, your failure to believe in yourself will prevent you from achieving your goals. Hence, take a look around. You will discover that individuals who succeed are those who have faith in their capabilities.

Imagine yourself on the starting block, the pool stretching out before you like an endless expanse of blue.

Take a deep breath, feeling the cool air fill your lungs. Close your eyes, and for a moment, let go of all distractions.

Picture yourself gliding through the water, your body moving with effortless grace. Feel the resistance of the water as you propel yourself forward, your limbs slicing through the surface. Hear the rhythmic whoosh of your arms and the gentle splash of your legs.

Visualize the finish line, a beacon of hope and victory. Sense the surge of adrenaline coursing through your veins as you pick up your pace, your heart pounding in your chest.

Open your eyes, and let the vivid image of your success linger in your mind. Carry this newfound confidence with you, and you will find yourself well on your way to achieving your goals.

Mentally, render it as real-world as possible.

Describe the experience in detail - what you wore, if the water was warm or cold, how hard you breathed, what sounds you heard, etc. Picture yourself finishing with a smile, feeling truly rewarded and happy to reach the goal.

See, that wasn't so bad! Remember to speak positively about yourself and value your worth. Be your own best friend rather than criticizing yourself when you mess up. Many think you should beat yourself up over mistakes, but self-compassion is important too.

Self-deprecation serves no purpose.

Remind yourself of your strengths. Stop immediately if you find yourself thinking negatively about yourself. By employing positive thinking, transform that remark into one that is uplifting.

For example, if you trip over something you didn't notice, instead of saying "I'm so clumsy," say "Oh no, I missed seeing that there. But I'll be more aware next time to avoid this."

Keep an action plan in writing, listing daily steps to reach goals. Include reward days for fun too. Make the plan suit your needs rather than others' advice. This control helps build lasting positivity and motivation.

Use a journal to record progress on short-term goals daily, and emotions doing certain activities. Do they help or hinder goals? If not helpful, visualize how you would prefer to feel instead while doing the task.

Regularly documenting and reviewing progress assists in cementing a constructive mindset over time.

You must certainly be truthful with yourself. Don't write anything you accomplished when you did not and avoid offering excuses. Although it is possible to deceive others, one can't deceive oneself.

Thus, I present a few practical and beneficial suggestions for your consideration.

With appropriate application, one will quickly discover that positive thinking can facilitate attaining desired outcomes.

Outstanding Positive Thinking Methods

When experiencing anger, frustration, disappointment, sadness, fear or nothing at all, the guiding influence of positive thinking is essential. While I don't assert that positive thinking operates miraculously, it is accurate to state that positive thinking grounded in reality can ultimately benefit all individuals.

Positive thinking can inspire tremendous hope and motivation to grow. But staying positive takes work - it's as much about limiting negativity as creating positivity. Here are 3 effective tips for maintaining an upbeat mindset:

1. Start a gratitude journal. Writing a few things you're grateful for every day directs focus to the bright side. Over time, this habit builds more positive thinking patterns.

2. Evaluate thoughts objectively. When negative self-talk arises, ask yourself - is this absolutely true? What evidence supports or

disputes it? Assessing accuracy avoids exaggerating downsides.

Discover the value of failure.

Failure is both discouraging and frustrating and difficult to manage; however, it also presents an opportunity to reassess one's approach and return with enhanced readiness. Learning to discover the silver lining in failure facilitates overcoming failure and its associated negative emotions.

Reflect on the lessons you've learned from your failures and consider whether they've contributed to your character development. What changes would you make for the future?

Capitalize on the situation by reframing failure as an opportunity to learn and a launching stone to subsequent success. This is an improvement over hunkering down, hoping that time will mend the wound.

A fresh perspective can significantly change an outlook; to achieve this, one must discover the positive in failure.

Retired, legendary basketball player Michael Jordan speaks for himself in a Nike advertisement:

As a player, I've missed over 9000 shots. I've dropped almost 300 games. 26 times, I've been given the chance to make the game-winning shot but failed. I've failed many times in my life, which is why I win now.

It would be a naive assumption to believe that Jordan's ascent to the pinnacle of the sport is solely due to his inherent aptitude. Indeed, during his formative years, he encountered many setbacks that even his basketball instructors struggled to disregard, such as his failure to attain the minimum height requirement. Despite this, he insisted. Years of perseverance, effort, practice and setbacks contributed to the development of the stellar star.

Consider the scenario where he is as readily defeated by failure as most of us are and no one has ever heard of him. It is indisputable that fate exercises its influence over all money, regardless of its value. Each time you regain your composure following a setback, you are likely one step closer to success than your rivals.

Orient your focus towards the positive aspects.

Learning to manage your attention is key to success.

An insightful statement attributed to William James, the first educator to offer a psychology course in the United States and an American philosopher, historian and psychologist, was found in his book The Principles of Psychology: "My experience is what I agree to attend to." In other words, your life is determined by the experiences you focus on.

An important part of managing attention is shifting it toward the positive when frustrated.

We always suffer emotionally in the present moment - where we put attention determines feelings now. Mastering ways to refocus thoughts on good experiences lets you temporarily block upsetting memories.

As you pay more attention to positive things, you start to see the world more optimistically. Performance improves and you become less aware of negatives around you.

So by purposefully focusing on uplifting aspects of life, you can boost mood, productivity and happiness over time through simple attention training.

Three stages are involved in shifting attention.

Disengaging from the current focus, transitioning to a different location and re-engaging with novel stimuli. Among these stages, disengaging from the present circumstance is the most arduous.

Almost everyone commits the mistake of being perpetually entangled in negative emotions.

I set the quote "Progress over perfection" as my computer wallpaper. Whenever I sit down to work and see those words, it reminds me not to criticize small mistakes.

I imagine my most encouraging friend looking over my shoulder as I type, telling me to stay patient with myself. Overthinking errors only slows momentum.

This visualization trick helps me gain calmer perspective. By picturing a wise advisor rather than my own inner critic judging work, imperfections seem less disastrous.

For instance, during the most difficult time of the day, try to visualize something that pleases you unrelated to the current situation.

This could include anticipating an upcoming event, indulging in delectable beverages or eating something delicious.

Positive emotions can counterbalance the negative sentiments that negative emotions induce. Creating opportunities to experience positive emotions is essential for overcoming negative emotions and developing a positive thought process.

How can opportunities to experience positive emotions be created?

Observing adorable infant animals, such as llamas and baby dolphins, may elicit positive emotions such as curiosity or affection. Is that not an uncomplicated method of amusement? One can engage in various amusing activities to combat negative emotions, such as reading a comic book or watching a video about huskies who inadvertently humiliated themselves.

Moreover, those humorous, joyful instances that elicit positive emotions persist longer than anticipated. Let me set an example: I enjoy practicing yoga tremendously and watching comedy shows and working and playing video games and tennis and teaching my students .

Each time I complete a challenging task, I am filled with immense pride and a recollection of my joy.

When confronted with minor and major setbacks, such as my cell phone screen being broken by accident or failing to pass editorial screening for publication, I recall the joyful moments I spent in my activists . This helps me combat the negative emotions that happen daily.

"Ten years ago, was the best time to plant a tree; the present is the second best time," according to an ancient Chinese proverb. As the saying goes, practice makes perfect; the instant you begin to move, that is precisely when you begin to change. Practicing positive thinking techniques is excellent for surmounting obstacles and improving self-perception.

Another thing I've learned from personal experience is that training your mind to think positively is difficult but well worth the effort, much like practicing yoga. Like exercising muscles, the more time you devote to cultivating positive thinking, the more robust it will become. It is normal to encounter negative thoughts; however, cultivating the habit of thinking positively equips you with a potent weapon to overcome them.

Positive thinking increases one's happiness and significantly enhances the quality of life in quantifiable ways.

HOW CAN YOU ASSIST IN IMPROVING YOUR MOOD?

We are susceptible to being influenced by our disposition. We engage in more conversation, seek out activities we enjoy and embark on new excursions when joyful.

Our emotions undoubtedly influence our behavior. When we feel depressed, we may withdraw from social interactions, neglect our physical well-being, and find it challenging to engage in activities that once brought us joy. Similarly, anger can manifest in outbursts of frustration, irritability, and an inclination to isolate ourselves from others.

While emotions play a significant role in shaping our actions, it's crucial to recognize that our thoughts are the driving force behind our emotions. Our perception of situations, our interpretation of events, and our beliefs about ourselves and the world around us determine how we feel.

Consider two individuals experiencing the same situation, such as a job rejection. One individual might view it as a setback, a temporary obstacle on their path to success. They might feel disappointed, but they also remain optimistic and determined to pursue their goals.

On the other hand, another individual might interpret the rejection as a personal failure, a reflection of their inadequacy. They might feel discouraged, defeated, and even worthless. Their perception of the situation has directly influenced their emotional response.

This connection between thoughts and emotions highlights the importance of cultivating positive thinking. By intentionally focusing on the positive aspects of our lives, engaging in self-compassion, and challenging negative self-talk, we can effectively manage our emotions and foster a more resilient mindset.

When we choose to view challenges as opportunities for growth, setbacks as learning experiences, and criticism as a source for improvement, we reframe our perceptions and transform our emotional responses.

In essence, our thoughts are the seeds from which our emotions blossom. By understanding this connection and intentionally nurturing positive thoughts, we empower ourselves to cultivate a more balanced, resilient, and optimistic outlook.

Often, individuals seek the assistance of professionals out of concern for their disposition. For instance, they wish they were cheerful or less angry.

Individuals may also consider seeking treatment if they are dissatisfied with their behaviors, including increased weeping, eating or sleeping.

Still, one's thoughts significantly influence one's emotions and actions.

Before pursuing the assistance of a therapist, the primary objective in attempting to enhance one's mood should be a transformation of one's mindset. A mentality is defined as a "fixed state of mind" by the Merriam-Webster dictionary.

Predicated on the phrase "fixed," When you adopt a rigid mindset towards situations, your thought processes lack flexibility, and you will react the same way you have historically or recently.

While this strategy may prove effective in most circumstances, it may not be the most effective when I am sad, anxious or angry.

Negative thoughts result in negative emotions and behaviors, precipitating a deteriorating spiral. The individual's emotional state may improve; however, their fixed mentality prevents them from perceiving such changes and adapting to the potential improvements.

It is not synonymous with "positive thinking" to change one's thinking. Positive thinking encompasses thoughts such as "Life is wonderful" and "I am well-liked by everyone." These notions are irrational; consequently, you will not accept them as true.

When attempting to change one's disposition through cognitive restructuring, it is most effective to recall instances that corroborate the desired thought while avoiding those that contradict it.

After reviewing the information, generate a new, realistic thought, such as "Although my brother and my best friend are angry with me, I still have parents and coworkers who care about me." Changing your mindset means changing how you think.

You have shifted from believing that "everyone hates me" to believing that "although my brother and my best friend are angry with me, there are still parents and coworkers who care about me."

While you may continue to experience sadness or distress due to your circumstances, your disposition will gradually improve, enabling you to persist in implementing modifications.

Like water undergoes treatment before consumption, one's thoughts should be treated before establishing permanent residence within the mind. You would not consume contaminated sewage water lest it make you sick; similarly, you should not allow negative notions to clog your mind like sewage water.

Subject your mind to a treatment procedure designed to expel all elements except those possessing the purest and highest frequency.

To accomplish this, you must convert negative thoughts into outcasts by cultivating so many positive emotions that any negative thoughts that may visit will feel out of place.

Adhere to these steps to force negative thoughts to convert or seek lodging elsewhere.

1- A concentrated drop of positivity:

An entire glass of polluted water can be purified with bleach. Similar to how a single intense positive emotion can eradicate many negative ones.

Consider the happiest moment that has ever happened in your existence. Visualize it in slow motion as a reel within your mind's screen while your eyes are closed. Rewind this reel for the day.

2-Opposites Don't Coexist:

Imagine your mind as a vast garden, where thoughts are the seeds you sow. Just as a gardener carefully selects the seeds they plant, you can control the thoughts that take root in your mind.

When you focus on positive thoughts, you create a fertile ground for optimism, resilience, and joy. Like delicate flowers, positive thoughts flourish in an environment of nurturing self-compassion and supportive beliefs.

Negativity, on the other hand, acts like a relentless weed, choking out the growth of positivity and draining your emotional energy. Just as a vigilant gardener removes weeds to protect their precious blooms, you must actively combat negative thoughts to safeguard your mental well-being.

The key to cultivating a positive mindset lies in recognizing the interconnectedness of thoughts and emotions. When you deliberately cultivate positive thoughts, you shift the trajectory of your emotions, fostering a sense of optimism and hope.

To counter the intrusion of negative thoughts, engage in a practice of self-inquiry. Ask yourself, "What is positive about the current situation?" This simple question invites you to reframe your perspective, seeking out the hidden gems of positivity that may have been obscured by negativity's shadow.

By consistently nurturing a stream of positive thoughts, you create a protective barrier against the onslaught of negativity. Just as a bountiful garden is a testament to the gardener's care, a mind brimming with positivity reflects the power of your conscious cultivation.

Embrace the transformative power of positive thinking, and you will discover a world of possibilities, where challenges are embraced as opportunities, setbacks are transformed into lessons, and criticism is seen as a catalyst for growth.

3-Anticipate A Positive Day:

Your day will unfold favorably due to your optimistic mindset. One should not wait for favorable circumstances to transpire before embracing positivity.

After cultivating a positive mindset, favorable circumstances will begin to transpire. Reaffirm the following: Today, something positive will happen. Anticipating it is analogous to anticipating the sun's rise at dawn.

4. Morning Script:

Each morning, mentally compose a script outlining the events that will transpire throughout the day. Speculate: What would my ideal day entail on this particular day? Allow yourself to envision everything transpiring following your desires momentarily. Keep in mind that positive outcomes occur in positive individuals.

5-Night Script:

Before retiring to sleep, mentally eliminate any portions of your day that evoke negative emotions. Enhance a portion of them. This is how. Enter your mind and separate an experience.

As the producer, revise any statements or actions you or others produced that you found objectionable. Your mind and your script comprise it. No one should inhabit it unless they are hospitable.

Maintaining a positive perspective is critical in a multitude of domains. Positive thinking increases productivity and quality, according to studies. An increase in positive emotions inherently fosters creativity, which consequently enhances performance. Your confidence will soar when you perform at your highest level, positively impacting every aspect of your personal and professional life.

Fear can impede one's progress and hinder the generation of productive thoughts. The apprehension of being exposed, disproven, or losing what we possess can impede our ability to make advantageous choices. If negative thinking results in erroneous judgment, then we become timid in the face of adversity.

When we perceive an opportunity as an unattainable challenge, we fail to capitalize on it and permit it to pass while most society progresses forward and upward. Adverse affective states such as fear, regret, anxiety, jealousy, anger and sorrow not only elicit profound physical manifestations but also exert a substantial influence on one's behavior in daily existence. Negative emotions have the potential to solidify poor decision-making patterns.

An enormous advantage of personal development is that it can encourage us to cultivate our positive attributes while diminishing those deemed less desirable. It can provide us with inner serenity and an overall improvement in our health, given that our emotions, values, attitudes, motivations and beliefs are all interconnected.

Let us examine some techniques for maintaining a positive outlook:

Set goals

Encouragement would not be necessary if life were effortless. Establishing consistent challenges and goals—such as learning a new language or engaging in a creative hobby—can, therefore, aid in the development of a disciplined, well-trained mind that will benefit you in different other endeavors.

Sustaining self-assurance and drive is critical for attaining sustained success. To attain long-term success, however, it is necessary to establish and achieve short-term goals! Providing a modest reward for yourself upon achieving each short-term objective will also maintain motivation.

Have faith in oneself.

This is of the utmost importance. Setting goals is meaningless if you lack confidence in your ability to accomplish them. Have faith that you are capable of succeeding. A minority of individuals achieve success by lacking confidence in themselves or their endeavors.

Visualization could be beneficial. Visualize yourself accomplishing your objective and experience the immeasurable gratification and happiness that accompany the accomplishment.

Respect yourself

Hold positive thoughts regarding oneself. Be kind to yourself as you would an esteemed companion. Make an effort to become your greatest supporter rather than your worst critic. Be conscious of any negative thoughts or words you may have about yourself. Replace these negative remarks with encouraging ones.

Developing a plan of action

After eliminating these negative thoughts, direct your attention toward creating an action plan that will be the cornerstone of your optimistic mindset. Incorporate reward days into the schedule to increase motivation.

Your plan should be individualized to accommodate your specific requirements. Customizing it will demonstrate that you have agency over your future. A well-defined plan of action will assist you in concentrating on the current undertaking. You will no longer feel directionless and impotent.

Maintain a journal

Maintain a daily journal in which you record your progress toward your goals. Also, record your feelings regarding yourself. Keeping track of your progress will undoubtedly assist in cultivating a positive mindset. Honesty is essential for this to succeed. If you deceive yourself, it is highly improbable that you will succeed in reaching your objective.

Adhering to these strategies is effective. You will rapidly develop a greater sense of optimism and appreciate life more. Implement the plan!

RECOGNIZING ADVERSE PATTERNS AND THE PRACTICAL IMPLICATIONS OF NEGATIVE INDIVIDUALS AND ENVIRONMENTS

Life is filled with many surprises for everyone. While a portion of these surprises are agreeable, others are not. Nevertheless, each occurrence reveals a fresh facet and people ought to internalize the lesson for the rest of their lives. Although professional accomplishments, recognition and success hold great importance, the individuals in one's personal life truly impact change.

The ability of others with a positive attitude to bestow joy upon you will assist you in living a successful existence.

Conversely, individuals with a negative outlook will disturb the equilibrium and harmony in one's existence. It is of the utmost importance to select the appropriate individuals.

Positive-minded individuals should be your constant search, whether in colleagues, peers, acquaintances or employers. Accurately distinguishing negative entities and individuals is critical, as it will facilitate the cultivation of a successful and harmonious existence.

It is unwise to invest time and energy in negative individuals. Individuals who are cynical and judgmental should be excluded from your life, as they don't contribute positively. At this moment, an essential inquiry arises within your mind.

How do you become aware that negative individuals are present in your life?

What exactly enables you to comprehend their existence?

Upon examination of the subsequent points, one can discern the most prominent indicators of negative-minded individuals.

Without a doubt, no one can survive in seclusion and solitude. As a social animal, human requires the companionship of others to function properly.

You must identify the right individuals at this juncture because associating with a toxic company will wreak havoc on your mental tranquility.

The subsequent elements will assist you in recognizing negativity and toxicity in the individuals in your vicinity. For a thorough understanding, consider the following factors:

1. Your companions have no regard for your presence.

Surrounding yourself with supportive and positive individuals is essential for personal growth and happiness. These individuals uplift you, encourage you to reach your full potential, and celebrate your successes.

On the other hand, detrimental relationships can drain your energy, dampen your spirit, and hinder your progress. These individuals may criticize you, belittle your accomplishments, and make you feel undervalued. Such relationships can negatively impact your self-esteem, confidence, and overall well-being.

It is crucial to recognize and avoid these detrimental connections. It may be challenging to sever ties with individuals who have been part of your life, but it is essential to protect your mental and emotional well-being.

Seek out relationships that nurture your growth, inspire your dreams, and bring joy to your life. Cultivate friendships with individuals who appreciate you for who you are, who support your endeavors, and who celebrate your victories.

Remember, the company you keep significantly impacts your overall well-being. Choose wisely, and you will create a supportive network that empowers you to thrive.

2. Greening with jealousy

The presence of envious individuals in your life can have a detrimental impact on your well-being and happiness. When surrounded by those who harbor jealousy and envy, you may experience emotional turmoil, leading to feelings of guilt, resentment, and self-doubt.

As you witness the achievements of others, envious individuals may project their own insecurities and unfulfilled desires onto you. Their negative energy can undermine your confidence and make you question your own accomplishments.

Envy is a destructive emotion that can poison relationships and hinder personal growth. It can lead to conflicts, misunderstandings, and a gradual erosion of trust.

To protect yourself from the harmful effects of envy, it is important to recognize and avoid associating with individuals who exhibit such traits. Surround yourself with supportive and encouraging people who celebrate your successes and uplift you during challenging times.

Remember, your worth is not determined by the opinions or actions of others. Embrace your accomplishments with pride and never let the envy of others diminish your sense of self-worth.

3. They desire for you to be changed.

It's important to strive to be accepted and loved for who you are. However, sometimes, the desire to fit in or be liked by others can lead to compromising your values and beliefs. It's important to remember that true friends will never try to change you into someone you're not.

If you find yourself constantly changing your behavior or opinions to please others, it's time to take a step back and reassess your relationships.

Are these people truly your friends, or are they just trying to mold you into someone they'll be more comfortable with?

True friends will accept you for who you are, flaws and all. They will support your dreams and encourage you to be the best version of yourself. They will also be honest with you, even when it's difficult, because they care about your well-being.

If you're lucky enough to have friends like this, cherish them. They are a rare and precious gift.

To find more genuine relationships, it's important to seek out people who share your values and interests. These are the people who will understand you and appreciate you for who you are.

Remember, it's better to have a few close friends who truly accept you than to have a large group of friends who only like you for who you pretend to be.

4. Change Adverse Behavior and Impulses

Similar to sports activities or any other process, it is evident that relating oneself to the fundamentals is essential to improve one's performance, irrespective of the subsequent actions taken.

Also, the foundation of effecting personal change lies within, utilizing one's beliefs, particularly those of the subconscious. Changing a concept is a domino effect; for instance, to prevent alcohol cravings, to prevent overeating from causing health problems or to prevent procrastination.

However, there are times when a behavior has resulted in complications that necessitate the assistance of a professional and the implementation of different techniques and strategies to return to one's natural, healthy self. Also, employing multiple modalities is often advantageous as they are mutually reinforcing. Essentially, there is no single method that is optimal for all individuals.

Therefore, if there is one fundamental principle that ought always to be applied, it is the influence of the subconscious mind, as it is the source of all problems that arose initially. Although Hippocrates, the father of medicine, once stated that the psyche and body are not separate entities, they must be treated simultaneously. Every change originates internally rather than externally.

Keep "self-help" in mind even though we seek the assistance of others during the process of self-healing. The self constitutes the most significant component of this process and any other that will provide us respite from our desires, behaviors or problems.

This timeless concept and truth have been utilized in every culture. Yet, it has been disregarded because "modern man" has been preoccupied with self-awareness, deliberate thought and the quest for comprehension. Nobody would be experiencing problems and be significantly happier and healthier if that were the case, but that is not how things operate.

The conclusive outcomes validate the adage "the proof is in the pudding." A plethora of case studies, research and testing conducted in hospitals, healthcare facilities and mental health studies, among others, demonstrate that the influence of the subconscious mind on individual thought processes, actions and outcomes can't be avoided.

There are instances in which the adage "something seems too good to be true" comes to pass as the actual product. However, this is no more true than the oxygen we breathe or the ground we walk upon when accessing the unconscious mind for answers, guidance and emotional, mental and physical transformations simply by sitting quietly and in solitude.

Like gravity, it suffices to recognize that it operates without understanding its mechanism. Unquestionably, belief is a potent factor.

Consider how restricted all individuals were whenever their beliefs obstructed the pursuit of absolute truths. Although the earth has never been flat and left-handed individuals have never been witches, your belief will make it so, at least for you, regardless of what others may say. Therefore, leverage the power of your thoughts, which has been at your disposal ever since man existed, to achieve greater happiness and health.

Emotions are transitory mental states; resist the urge to allow them to destroy you irrevocably. Scholars have determined that emotions significantly influence our state of being.

Negative emotions harm the body, whereas positive emotions have beneficial effects. Understanding the nature of emotions and their physiological and psychological impacts is essential for effectively managing and exerting control over negative thoughts and feelings.

Emotions and feelings play a significant role in our daily lives. Humans often exhibit emotions. A further elucidation of the negative and positive emotions through which they manifest their emotions is forthcoming in this chapter. Behaviorism is also associated with emotions. Introverted individuals are less likely to exhibit their emotions than extroverts.

We experience joy when we finally accomplish something we have long yearned for. On the contrary, we experience sadness when we cannot obtain our preferred item.

Consider that you win a BMW in the lottery. How will you experience yourself?

Seated or joyful?

Certainly, delighted?

Consider the scenario in which you recently completed the CA examination and are awaiting the results. This time, you believed you would pass but received an unfavorable result. How might you feel?

Delighted or Sad?

Certainly, sadness will induce different negative thoughts that harm your body.

Negative thoughts and emotions must be learned to manage and control to live a happy, stress-free existence. Consider that your father has reprimanded you for an mistake you have committed and that you are perpetually perplexed as to why.

One may potentially jeopardize one's health by fixating excessively on a negative incident. You should, therefore, acquire the ability to control negative thoughts. We can achieve a positive outcome by regulating our negative thoughts and emotions.

Before anything else, it is essential to distinguish between negative and positive emotions. Also, this blog will explain the impact of negative and positive emotions on our well-being. We have provided a few suggestions on how to manage negative emotions effectively.

Scholars have categorized emotions into two primary components.

Positive or good emotions.

Favorable emotions, including but not limited to love, pleasure, hope, pride, motivation, confidence and optimism, make an individual better.

These emotions increase our receptivity and creativity. Positive emotions stimulate the intellect and heart.

A well-known proverb states, "Positive emotions produce wise, kind and humble individuals, while negative thoughts produce foolish, unkind and arrogant individuals." The success mantra further asserts that associating positive emotions with desired outcomes increases the likelihood of attaining those goals.

The relationship between health and emotion is profound. A healthy diet and regular exercise do not solely determine our health. Positive thinking is beneficial to both the body and the mind.

Scholars have established that consistent exposure to positive emotions is vital for preserving optimal health. Laughter is the most effective remedy for decreasing the release of stress hormones like cortisol and epinephrine.

Negative or Bad Emotions

Negative emotions make life unpleasant and challenging. We often experience anxiety or depression when we are sad, angry or frustrated. Stress, melancholy, uncontrollable anger and other similar issues are prevalent emotional challenges that affect a significant number of individuals. For instance, individuals experience negative sentiments when subjected to inappropriate behavior.

Negative emotions, such as anger, hatred, and tension, can cloud our judgment and lead to poor decision-making. When we are consumed by these emotions, we may act impulsively and without considering the consequences. This can lead to a number of negative outcomes, such as regret, conflict, and damage to our relationships.

It is important to be aware of our emotional triggers and to develop strategies for managing them. This may include relaxation techniques, such as deep breathing or meditation, or finding healthy outlets for our emotions, such as exercise or journaling.

The ability to regulate our negative emotions is not only important for making sound decisions, but it is also essential for our overall well-being. When we are able to manage our emotions effectively, we are less likely to experience stress, anxiety, and depression.

If you are struggling to manage your negative emotions, it may be helpful to talk to a therapist or counselor. They can teach you coping mechanisms and help you develop a plan for managing your emotions.

Remember, you are not alone. Many people struggle with negative emotions, and there is help available. With effort and support, you can learn to manage your emotions and make better decisions for yourself.

Recognizing the Impact of Negative Thoughts on Our Well-Being.

Stress induces the release of the hormone cortisol in the organism. Negative emotions can give rise to a range of significant physical and mental challenges, including but not limited to headaches, irritations, insomnia, excessive fatigue, digestive issues, compromised immunity, memory lapses and learning disabilities.

Regardless of our mood (happy or depressed), we must maintain emotional control. Particularly and specifically, negative emotions require the utmost caution when it comes to handling.

Negative thoughts impair the operation of the intellect. Negative impulses include hurting oneself or others, seeking vengeance and so forth. Emotions should not dictate our lives; instead, we should control them.

How Can Negative Thoughts Be Restrained?

One can achieve happiness by transforming negative emotions and beliefs into positive ones. A game of "acceptance and non-acceptance" is at stake. A straightforward scientific principle underpins the generation of both negative and positive emotions. Negative thoughts are simple to manage and control if we glean their essential message from the following examples.

Example 1: We experience anxiety when someone performs an action in a manner that we don't approve of and refuse to accept. On the contrary, we maintain our tolerance if we acknowledge it.

Example 2: Jealousy ensues naturally when an individual possesses an item that we lack and refuses to acknowledge its existence. If we acknowledge that we lack the item, we should strive diligently and commit ourselves to attaining it. Doing so allows us to exert control over negative thoughts, gain inspiration and undoubtedly attain the desired level through diligent effort.

Example 3: If we have been emotionally wounded by someone and are not yet prepared to embrace it. Constantly pondering how the other person caused us pain leads to feelings of hatred. Nonetheless, negative thoughts can be managed, provided that we can accept the hurtful nature of the individual. This assists us in forgiving the individual as well.

Negative or positive emotions aren't caused by "someone" or "something," as is evident from this. Our "acceptance" or "non-acceptance" is completely irrelevant. Negative and positive emotions are associated with the terms mentioned above.

Before being troubled by negative thoughts and emotions, reflecting on the underlying causes compelling us to resist accepting certain situations is critical. Once the causes have been investigated, non-acceptance can be transformed into acceptance. This enables the transformation of negative emotions into positive ones and the regulation of negative thoughts.

SIMPLIFIED METHODS FOR CONFRONTING NEGATIVE THOUGHTS

Our society places considerable emphasis on the efficacy of positive thinking. The law of attraction is constantly discussed, which states that positive beliefs result in positive experiences. It also operates in the opposite direction.

According to this law, negative thinkers often manifest negative life experiences. Other manifestations of this concept include faith, the law of sowing and reaping and self-fulfilling prophecies. Notwithstanding the perspective one adopts, the law remains valid and irreversible. This evidence has been present in my life.

Therefore, the straightforward resolution is maintaining a positive mindset and engaging in positive beliefs. The difficulty lies in the fact that eliminating negative beliefs is difficult. A considerable number of those thoughts become deeply ingrained in one's consciousness.

Despite your desire to eliminate them and maintain positive thoughts, it is simple for negative thoughts to impede your progress. At times, notwithstanding one's diligent efforts, it is possible to succumb to negative thoughts and permit them to impede progress toward desired goals.

Therefore, the issue is how to eliminate these negative thoughts. Based on my research and effort to eliminate my negative thoughts, I have uncovered the following recommendations, which I am pleased to share. Three methods can be implemented to facilitate the elimination of negative thoughts.

They might differ from some of the more conventional ones you have encountered, such as cultivating a greater smile or engaging in meditation. While the tips mentioned are effective and beneficial, I would like to present alternative suggestions that are more likely to stimulate thought and leave a lasting impression.

1. Avoid resisting negative impulses.

Have you ever noticed that resistance only results in their persistence? The same holds for negative beliefs. Their number and intensity seem to increase directly to your efforts to eliminate and combat them.

To avoid this, the opposite action is taken. Negative thoughts can be acknowledged and permitted. This may appear to be a waste of time, particularly since your objective is to eliminate them.

Nevertheless, by recognizing and embracing these thoughts, one can avert the opposition that results from attempting to eradicate them with force. I almost immediately experience a greater sense of tranquility when I do this. Consequently, my ability to think more positively is enhanced, enabling me to think more accurately. The same will happen to you.

2. Remain mindful of your agency.

Thoughts can quickly consume you and spiral out of control like a runaway locomotive. Despite this, it is essential to remember that you have complete authority over your own beliefs. Furthermore, what are your thoughts? They are mere mental images or words that pass through the mind.

3. Positive displacement.

As previously stated, negative concepts can't be expelled through force.

You must instead eliminate them and progressively substitute them with positive beliefs.

Consider an entire container of mud. To transform the glass from soiled to clean, it is not feasible to dispose of the entire quantity of grime simultaneously. Clean water must be poured steadily through the glass.

Clean water ultimately supplants the filth. As you proceed with this process, the glass becomes entirely pristine. The same holds for our beliefs. Progressively supplant pessimistic thoughts with more optimistic ones until the optimistic ones predominate.

This can be accomplished via positive affirmations, visualization and similar techniques. This is effective because releasing negative emotions prevents you from exacerbating the situation.

Ultimately, your positive beliefs motivate you to take the necessary steps toward achieving your goals. Undoubtedly, one can devise additional strategies to eliminate negative beliefs. Please feel at liberty to provide feedback and offer additional recommendations. Surely, they can also be of great assistance.

The approaches elucidated in this discourse are those I have discovered to be the most productive and possess the most substantial capacity to facilitate sustained progress in eliminating the detrimental thoughts that have impeded your progress thus far.

You have absolute control over your mind, one of the few things in existence and possesses the greatest power in the universe. Regardless of the degree to which one harbors a negative outlook, exerting some effort to replace negative thoughts with positive ones will fundamentally change cognitive processes.

It is essential not to become disheartened if you continue cultivating positive thoughts despite making a concerted effort to improve but failing to observe results. This transformation doesn't happen immediately. Your mind is hardwired to generate negative thoughts naturally; therefore, transforming it will require consistent effort.

A book on the subject is one of the most effective methods to begin the process of replacing negative thoughts with positive ones. Explore any bookstore's Religion and Spirituality or Self-Help sections to locate some books that will be an excellent introduction to mental transformation.

It is critical to not only read the book but to read it methodically and put into practice what you find out. Certain highly influential books on mind-body rehabilitation can assist you in attaining a greater sense of mental and spiritual wholeness, enhancing your thought processes.

Eventually, you will perceive the positive before the negative by speaking positively to yourself. You must first identify the negative concepts that traverse your mind daily before you can accomplish that.

Engaging in the practice of documenting each negative thought experienced while at home, at work or in any other setting would serve as a beneficial exercise. Identifying them may become second nature long after you have been pondering that manner. Consequently, this may make the task more challenging.

Rewrite each negative thought you recorded into positive sentences after the day. Then, aloud recite the aforementioned positive statements to yourself. By engaging in this exercise daily, you will develop the ability to recognize and transform negative thoughts and statements into positive ones.

Positive thinking is among the most prevalent characteristics of cheerful individuals. Constantly dwelling on negative thoughts is harmful to one's physical and mental health; therefore, it is worthwhile to devote some time to mind-body rehabilitation by transforming one's thoughts.

We all help our peers realize their dreams through our thoughts. Thoughts are essential to achieving accomplishment. It is a fundamental component of achievement. It has been observed since ancient times that individuals who have progressed in life tend to possess the most capable minds. He improved matters for the nation and society.

Often, it is observed that the mind's thinking generates concepts. The mind can be developed through education, observation and hearing, among other things; however, some individuals are born with an intelligent mind. Mental reasoning is vitally essential to us.

A successful outcome results from a well-functioning mind; conversely, failure results from an unproductive mind. Consciously maintain mental acuity and vigilance. What are you contemplating and what is the subject of your thoughts?

Perhaps your focus is diverting from the intended objective due to preoccupation with unrelated subjects. Those who deviate and cause disruption must exercise self-control and monitor their Dainik activities.

When you are conversing with yourself, the subject is serious. It indicates that you have a mental illness. "You achieve success with a negative attitude. It is called Luck. But you achieve success in life with a positive attitude. It is called truly an achievement."

Individuals who possess a brilliant intellect by nature or birth are considered a divine gift. Individuals of this nature achieve achievement in their lives.

Preventing further obstacles is imperative for attaining success in one's existence. Such a mind generates positive ideas and retains the greatest capacity for thought.

Whether by nature or by inheritance, they possess the keys to success. They don't increase their level of force to eliminate the challenges associated with achieving success because they are divine favors.

Those with a senseless mentality by nature or birth are known as "stupid." Such individuals never achieve achievement in life. Nearly 30% of these individuals achieve accomplishment in life but encounter greater obstacles.

Occasionally, this happens so that their losses exceed their successes. If you desire success despite having a senseless mind, maintain constant vigilance and exercise caution regarding the activities in your immediate surroundings. For them, concern and awareness are merely prerequisites for success.

If one aspires to achieve achievement in life, it is irrelevant to whom one considers. Whether you are brilliant or dumb, you would need to become active.

Never forget these factors to achieve success in life.

- Complete all duties punctually
- Be vigilant and cautious
- Maintain a courteous demeanor
- Avoid harboring a haughty spirit
- Remain focused on the objective
- Put forth the effort
- Read success-oriented journals and periodicals.
- Mind and body wellness are essential.
- Maintain fewer arguments on target.

Remember the principles mentioned above if you wish to reach the pinnacle of your dream in the future. Start strategizing to attain your goals while bearing in mind the following considerations. You would certainly achieve achievement in your endeavors.

When enthusiastic about undertaking an endeavor, positive thoughts often enter their consciousness.

Success and happiness are invariably observed to be the outcomes of positive thinking in an individual's existence. They maintain a positive outlook. Positive thinking is the pinnacle of achievement.

Positive thoughts contribute to one's prosperity. It often happens to the mind after observing, comprehending or reading about another individual's accomplishments. Positive thinking serves as the fundamental foundation for achieving success.

Certain individuals perceive their dream of prosperity during the day, while others perceive it at night. Individuals who visualize accomplishment throughout the day have nothing but positive thoughts. Individuals who dream of triumph at night are more prone to conflict.

Negative thoughts often arise in further debate regarding a particular target. It originates primarily in the psyche of a genius. Because brilliant individuals consider their objective from a negative and positive perspective, they risk missing their intended objective if they don't choose the proper path to success.

Negative thoughts lead individuals astray and endow them with a life of misery after accumulating in one's consciousness. You deteriorate both mentally and physically. It poses a challenge to achieving accomplishment.

If you cannot make the right choice because more negative thoughts surround you, eliminate those thoughts.

To conclude, you are becoming entangled in a predicament. Visit tranquil and picturesque locales such as parks, zoos, beaches, museums and historical sites; avoid congested and noisy areas.

You should endeavor to clear your mind of all plans and notions by deleting or forgetting them. One day you must abandon your plan and resume your existence. You would then need to meet successful individuals relevant to your plan.

HOW TO DOMINATE OVER NEGATIVE THOUGHTS

The primary consequence of negative thinking is the experience of negative emotions and thoughts, which diminish one's confidence rather than enhance it. Having a negative internal dialogue with yourself could impede your self-assurance and hinder your ability to achieve your utmost capabilities.

A lack of sleep, common cold symptoms, fatigue, tension and hunger are all potential triggers for negative self-talk. Depression often arises as a consequence of negative pondering in isolation. Insecurity and a low sense of self-worth result from unfavorable perceptions.

You develop the sense that your existence lacks meaning and purpose. Psychologists have also identified negative thinking as a contributing factor to obsessive-compulsive disorder (OCD), persistent concern, anxiety and depression. This hostility also exerts a substantial influence on the human brain, as research indicates that engaging in negative thinking may heighten the susceptibility to dementia.

Most Persistent Negative Thoughts

1. An oversimplification

One example is concluding one's existence from a single unfortunate incident or circumstance such as "I can't do anything well because I received such poor grades on my physics exam!".

2. Labeling

Labeling is attributing a designation to oneself or another individual while neglecting to acknowledge the veracity underlying that designation.

"I'm such a loser; I'm not great in sports or school," or academically, "I didn't have anything to contribute to the discourse." Completely nothing fails to intrigue me.

A form of negative thinking known as emotional reasoning happens when an individual holds a belief and automatically assumes it is true. For instance, experiencing loneliness and erroneously believing that "No one wants to be with me because I'm lonely."

3. Predicting futures

Assuming the worst in every circumstance diminishes the opportunity to savor the present and increases the probability of adverse events.

For example, the thought might be: "If I ask that person for help, they'll just say no and make me feel unimportant!" When my mind goes to dramatic negative places, it's tedious and pointless to listen to.

4. Ignoring positive aspects

Positive aspects of the day were reduced to their bare necessities through unethical meditation. We disregard any information contradicting our pessimistic perception of ourselves or our circumstances. I performed admirably on that particular examination because I was extremely fortunate.

5. Catastrophizing

Have you ever contemplated the following: "My humiliation will kill me if I am not admitted to this college?" If so, your inner dialogue may contain catastrophizing language. By doing so, you are exaggerating the issue.

6. Thought delay

Neglecting the many benefits in favor of fixating exclusively on the drawbacks. One example is fixating on a solitary negative comment despite the instructor providing many positive and motivational messages.

7. Customization

A pervasive sense of self-blame characterizes anxiety of this nature in all circumstances. I conceived the following: "Everyone would make jokes about me regarding the occasion I stumbled over. I am aware of ".

When using imperative verbs such as "should" and "must," it is critical to consider the expectations placed upon you.

For illustration, "I shouldn't feel anxious while presenting a presentation in front of the class."

"Once you replace negative thoughts with positive thoughts, you'll recover your faith in this colorful, beautiful globe."

What measures can be implemented to cease or prevent the occurrence of these negative, purposeless thoughts?

To cultivate positive emotions in place of negative ones, one must develop an awareness of their emotions. It has been established that there are circumstances in which the approach of a black hole can't be detected.

It is advisable to pause before forming an opinion, expressing it, or passing judgment on any notion. Doing so would prompt one to consider whether such actions induce feelings of depression, negativity or melancholy. You must be capable of controlling these emotions if they are genuinely yours; otherwise, they should not be detrimental to you.

Listed below are some techniques for enhancing your disposition:

In the end, they are merely "thoughts." It doesn't make them true: It is essential to remember that visualizing certain fearful events doesn't automatically guarantee their actualization.

The purpose of pondering is to provide visual gratification so one can form personal opinions by utilizing one's human potential. Self-praising is the most effective course of action. Compensating for the negativity generated internally is akin to excavating one's tomb.

Pay close attention to how you feel:

Experience any sorrow you might feel. However, resist the temptation to delude that this is your permanent state of mind. You can prevent these awful emotions from becoming your reality by resisting the urge to be consumed by them.

Perform a kind deed for yourself: Discover joy in the smallest things. Also, you may encounter something humorous.

Have a night of complete slumber. Practice judicious eating. Start moving: Developing self-compassion contributes to a heightened sense of internal well-being.

Donate an expression of appreciation for your blessings: Every single one of us has a great deal for which to be thankful. What do you hold in high regard?

Enhance your interpersonal skills:

Stated this is an additional expression of the adage "build the neighborhood you desire." Invest time in companionship, family and acquaintances. Select the religion that fulfills your needs the most. Join a group or crew. Start investigating a new hobby.

When you comprehend negative affectivity, negative notions will become irrelevant. Moreover, therapy for negative thinking disorders enables you to concentrate on regulating negative emotions and finding happiness in the smallest of pleasures.

As an alternative to thinking, "We are departing to have a tough time adjusting to our existing situation," contemplate, "We will see some disputes in our livelihood condition but we will come up with a resolution that we will both be happy with."

Avoid acting as the victim. You are accountable for the life you give birth to.

One might argue that I was trapped in the method I was observing and executing but even if the circumstances surrounding our means of subsistence become unbearable, there is always a way out. I will consistently possess the agency to effectuate change when necessary.

Be of assistance to someone.

Distinguish yourself from the situation and demonstrate benevolence towards another individual. I, for one, resolved to prepare a serving of food to support charities. Engaging in charitable work diverted my attention and improved my overall mood.

Remember that nobody is flawless and permit yourself to progress.

It is easy to fixate on one's flaws; therefore, I felt terrible using this technique and ruined our weekend. Moving forward, the only thing I can do now is learn from my mistakes. Certainly, I don't wish to experience another weekend in that manner.

Sing.

My inability to commit words to memory may be why I don't find playing enjoyable, but I feel better whenever I sing. Toning serves as a manifestation of our thoughts, which provides an extraordinary anti-anxiety effect.

Please enumerate five items for which you are currently grateful.

Being grateful for what one already possesses is facilitated by being obliged. The following is a list of the things that I am grateful for: my cats, my physical health, a six-week trip to Asia, a new yoga class that I will be instructing and an impending lab biopsy for my mother.

Read inspiring quotations.

As a memento to remain constructive, I enjoy placing Post-It notes with optimistic quotation marks on my computer, refrigerator door and mirror. Also, a quotation attributed to an unidentified author was recited during my meditation class.

USE POSITIVE THOUGHTS TO BRING YOUR DREAMS TO LIFE

In the same way that human beings are composed of a bodily structure comprising tendons and ligaments, they also possess a cognitive organ that necessitates the same level of care as the body to preserve optimal health and wellness. The practice of positive thinking can instantly change one's lifestyle.

Our bodies are vital organs that require strict attention and maintenance; if they are negatively impacted, our lives can be drastically and unhappily changed. Those with hypertension must be mindful of their dietary choices, engage in daily physical activity or take lengthy walks to increase their body's vitality and activity. It is not prudent to wait for medical examinations to determine our condition. We must exercise control and initiative.

Our human brain can profoundly change our way of life and our relationships with the world. Suppose one lacks awareness of a negative thought entering their consciousness.

In that case, they will fail to recognize that it will inevitably give rise to additional negative thoughts. Once one focuses on this pessimistic trend, everything appears hopeless, melancholy and hopeless once more, as if one had succumbed to the deception and purchased it.

How often have you observed the pessimistic outlook on life exhibited by others—peers who are perpetually critical of everyone and everything—and, after some time, you realized that you were succumbing to the same behavior?

Unknowingly, negativity can be highly contagious; it is exceedingly simple to become collectively influenced by this unconscious domain. Over time, this detrimental cognitive pattern will have an impact on both one's health and personality. Life will inevitably become a nightmare if we maintain a pessimistic outlook on the world. Without exception, our expectations will be unfulfilled and everything will appear unfair.

It should come as no surprise that a negative person approaches a problem differently than a positive person; the contrast is night and day. An optimistic individual would confront the issue with assurance, viewing it not as a negative circumstance but rather as a chance to develop personally or professionally.

Also, they acknowledge the potential inability to rectify or resolve the situation; however, this notion would remain at the forefront of their minds and not penetrate their thoughts.

An individual with a pessimistic outlook would perceive this issue as lamentable or perhaps unfixable. Due to their inability to perceive potential outcomes, they would ordinarily withdraw into depression and close their minds.

All of this negativity has a devastating effect on our emotions, lowering the frequency of our energetic vibration to the point where it destroys our immune system, allowing viruses and diseases to penetrate our bodies unprotected. This phrase is not esoteric; it pertains to facts and science you can independently investigate.

Although negative thoughts are detrimental to our well-being, they are unavoidable. If you remain in this destructive emotional state for an extended period, you will develop pessimism, depriving you of health and pleasure; therefore, we must be aware of the techniques for quickly escaping this state.

Here are eight empowering suggestions for banishing negative thoughts and becoming a joyful person.

1. Allow yourself time to reflect positively and locate a comfortable place.

One may reflect upon the individual, occasion or instance from the past that brought them joy.

2. Regulating one's breathing through the gradual inhalation of deep breaths facilitates the elimination of negative thoughts and the accumulation of tension.

3. Maintain your time by engaging in activities that bring you joy, such as running, viewing movies, participating in sports, reading or similar pursuits. This will generate mental space that is conducive to negative thinking.

4. Shift your attention from the negative aspect to the positive experiences that bring you joy in life.

5. Confront your beliefs by reframing them. For instance, one should refrain from self-deprecating on a negative work day by affirming, "My work stinks!" rather than the more constructive, "My work is perpetually fraught with challenges that allow me to develop."

6. Association counts. You should surround yourself with positive-thinking individuals and share your struggles with them. However, avoiding associating with negative individuals is advisable, as they drain your positive energy and reinforce your negative beliefs.

7. Assist an individual in a more precarious circumstance than your own. This will cause you to reconsider the notion that your life is terrible when it is an excellent one compared to another person's.

8. Prohibit using negative words in conversation; substitute for them at all times with positive ones. Also, this will foster a positive environment for those around it.

Your manner of thinking will determine your worldview. It determines your level of success, happiness and overall quality of existence. Maintaining a positive outlook has a profound impact on one's existence.

BREAKING FREE FROM NEGATIVITY AND CHALLENGING LIMITING BELIEFS

Negative thoughts and ideas that are held in the subconscious constitute limiting beliefs. Most of these beliefs are formed during one's childhood and throughout one's existence. They are considered limiting because they harm your personal development and success.

To surmount one's false beliefs, it is imperative to acknowledge, embrace and transform said beliefs into constructive ones. This will empower you to develop a new set of beliefs that will assist you in conquering timidity and despondency.

Ideas and convictions that are limiting in nature are often acquired through formative years and life experiences. At times, one's actions that they perceive as good may appear to others as bad; conversely, others may perceive your actions as bad. To put it simply, each person possesses unique perspectives and convictions that are distinct from our own.

These beliefs are constructed through personal experience. We adhered to and complied with our parents' directives during our youth. Disobeying their regulations may result in disciplinary action, including possible weeklong grounding. This experience ingrained and solidified that disobedience to one's parents results in retribution. A person bullied by larger peers may suspect something is amiss with them.

The current you is the result of every life experience and set of beliefs that you have held. Individuals with a history of shyness or social awkwardness may have encountered situations in which they were embarrassed or prevented from displaying their true selves in front of an audience.

Regardless, these self-restrictive beliefs prevent you from attaining the success and fulfillment you aspire to be. Escape from your detrimental cycle and activate your authentic capabilities and latent strengths.

First, identify your personal beliefs.

Acknowledging and emphasizing one's ideologies constitutes an initial stride towards surmounting limiting beliefs. Understanding one's negative or positive beliefs leads to a profound sense of self-discovery and heightens one's consciousness regarding life's goals, values and ethics.

Secondly, accept them.

It is now time to embrace and cherish your beliefs once you have become aware of them.

Every individual holds certain beliefs for a reason; therefore, if you recall your limiting beliefs and the circumstances surrounding their formation, ingest those memories, come to terms with the reality that they happened and let go of them all.

Thirdly, transform your limiting beliefs into strengths.

The reason why limiting beliefs are formed is intentional. While the majority might understand it, it has the potential to teach us valuable lessons that could change the course of our lives.

By acknowledging and embracing these erroneous convictions, we can transform them into forces that empower us to achieve freedom. Having to relinquish all our burdens reminds us that improvement is possible and that hope remains.

Your false beliefs are designed to give you the fortitude and enlightenment necessary to defend yourself and achieve any goal you set for yourself. Changing one's beliefs can be very frustrating, but mastering these three straightforward steps for surmounting limiting beliefs can discover intrinsic pleasure.

Methods for Recognizing Your Limiting Beliefs

Limiting beliefs may manifest either consciously or unconsciously.

The identification of one's limiting beliefs can be achieved through the practice of thought observation. What do you commit to memory as a daily mantra? Which forms of negative self-talk do you engage in mentally?

You are most likely to recognize your limiting beliefs when you experience feelings of stagnation, obstruction, unhappiness or discontentment. What thoughts cross your mind during such times? That you lack sufficient quality? Or perhaps you are unable to do it due to _____. Perhaps you feel too _____ to attempt it.

One can discern their limiting beliefs in the justifications and pretexts they provide for their inability to progress in various aspects of life.

Fear, reluctance, lack of confidence, sorrow, discontentment, unhappiness, unworthiness, undeservingness, guilt, discouragement, demotivation and pessimism are the most prevalent emotions linked to limiting beliefs. Your beliefs are mirrored in your emotions. A bodily response to a thought is the expression of an emotion.

One reinforces the emotion linked to a negative thought by conjuring that thought. Continued self-criticism will likely result in feelings of undeservingness and a reluctance to take action. Maintaining this pattern will result in forming a habit subsequently restricting your progress.

Through the process of tracing your thoughts back, you will discover that they originate concerning your beliefs. Thoughts are determined by the self-perception and perception of the world that an individual holds.

Identifying conscious limiting beliefs is relatively simple; however, what transpires when these beliefs are concealed within the subconscious mind and remain undetected?

Identifying subliminal beliefs is as simple as examining one's life and noting all the areas where progress appears elusive despite exerting maximum effort. An obvious disparity exists between your current location and your desired destination.

Typically, this indicates a subliminal belief (which you likely adopted in your youth) and this antiquated program operates in the background without your knowledge. This subliminal belief will continue to oppose you unless you change it if it is not constructive.

Once you have identified the beliefs that don't support you, cultivate self-awareness regarding your decisions, routines, conduct, sentiments, thoughts and convictions. Although it requires consistent effort, the result will be well worth it.

The Power of Eliminating Limiting Beliefs to Create the Life of Your Dreams

Self-limiting beliefs are the most significant barrier to creating a wonderful existence. A self-limiting belief is an individual's conviction that their progress, abilities, resources, intellect, time or opportunities are somehow constrained.

Unfortunately, many people stay held back by their own limiting beliefs, never tapping into their huge potential.

A limiting belief is a negative story we buy about ourselves that restricts what we think we can do. These beliefs embed so deep that we rarely question if they are true. We act like they're facts, even in important times, when there's no proof they're right.

Therefore, eliminating these limiting beliefs should be a simple task; recognize their occurrence and choose to disregard them; our dilemma is resolved without further ado. Sadly, the issue's magnitude would be different if eliminating limiting beliefs were that simple.

Often, limiting beliefs are established during the formative years.

Consider a parent who lavishes their children with attention and attends to every need without allowing them to do so independently.

In such a scenario, the child may develop an aversion to responsibility as an adult and be unmotivated to change their behavior, as it will appear as though they have always been this way.

Assigning children to rigid roles can also result in the development of limiting beliefs. For instance, a child labeled as "shy" may persist in fearing social gatherings due to the habit of perceiving themselves in that way.

Similarly, a child who is considered "the jock" may avoid academic endeavors because doing so contradicts their long-held self-perception of their own identity and societal expectations.

Identifying limiting beliefs consciously is the initial step.

Like shadows, these beliefs can undermine you unnoticed; bring them into the light of day to ensure a fair fight. However, beware that limiting beliefs don't always masquerade as "identity" and are not always blatant and easily flushed out: "I'm not the type of person who."

If an individual labeled a "shy person" sincerely desires to engage in social interactions and establish connections with others, considering the situation objectively can be beneficial. There is no concrete barrier and nothing to lose, so why not try it?

The reward in this scenario is particularly substantial: the ability to relinquish the "shy person" persona. Putting aside our limiting beliefs can empower us to become more resilient.

Reflect thoughtfully on your aspirations and goals. Are there any concrete, logical impediments that prevent you from attaining them? While such obstacles may not be substantial, they don't necessarily have to be.

If the justifications include something like "That simply doesn't reflect my character," you should reconsider your stance. However, suppose the obstacle is something you genuinely desire and there is no physical obstruction. In that case, you can accomplish anything you set your mind to.

Constantly limiting beliefs prevents others from reaching their full potential. Don't be one of them; instead, delve into your self-beliefs and surmount them; you'll discover that your potential soars!

How Limiting Beliefs Constrain Life

Our beliefs serve as the bedrock for our identity, thoughts, words, actions and ultimately, how the world manifests itself. Nevertheless, we restrict our lives when we hold limiting beliefs.

Involvements in relationships.

Limiting beliefs can have a significant impact on interpersonal relationships. Holding beliefs regarding what is permissible, unacceptable or "bad" for the relationship can cause complications.

For instance, suppose you believe your partner should not allow you to see an ex-partners because it would be "bad" for the relationship. However, you fail to recognize that your partner genuinely cherishes you.

Various factors may contribute to the maintenance of a relationship with an ex-spouse. For instance, are children involved? Does your partner provide alimony to their ex-spouse? Was the breakup mutual?

While this doesn't imply continued love, it does indicate that they are maintaining a functional relationship for the benefit of whatever holds them together. However, if you believe they are "up to no good," you will reinforce that perception by seeking out circumstances that support that view.

Workplace Employment.

The extent to which one restricts their beliefs regarding employment can significantly impact their decision to remain in a particular position or pursue multiple career changes. It is possible to remain in a job that one despises because it is the "right thing to do" or because one believes there are no other viable options.

Fear, merely an additional belief, can also severely restrict one's life. It can prevent one from pursuing new educational opportunities, returning to school or initiating career changes.

Progress in Education.

Regarding education, we all impose certain constraints on what we deem acceptable. Suppose you chose not to attend college immediately after high school or dropped out.

The same company has employed you for ten years and has been contemplating returning to school to earn a degree but has refrained from doing so due to the belief that you are "too old," "have forgotten everything," or "won't make the grade."

It's normal to have forgotten some things from school because you don't apply them anymore; that doesn't make you less intelligent; rather, it's a normal part of the process. However, your beliefs prevent you from progressing, which keeps you in the same position you are in.

The spirit of creativity

The expression "Think outside the box" is widely recognized and even Taco Bell incorporates it into their slogan (Think Outside the Bun). However, many individuals have become so accustomed to the routine that they fail to recognize how they constrain their creative potential. They believe they must adhere to established parameters.

Should you awaken tomorrow without that morning coffee? Would that coffee derail your entire day? Would you be able to function normally? While physically unaffected, you might not be able to function normally, and you probably would be psychologically affected because it would be outside of your normal daily routine and you would likely perceive yourself as being off.

Regaining creativity in one's life necessitates a modification of established routines, engaging in impromptu activities, deviating from predetermined patterns consistently, and discovering a resurgence of creative inspiration.

You can change your reality by modifying your beliefs. Invest some time examining your beliefs and asking, "Why do I hold this conviction?"

Subsequently, inquire whether this belief aligns with my aspirations for my life."The answer to that question is typically "no." However, if it is "yes," you possess the chance to modify that belief regarding the matters that bolster your aspirations, thereby augmenting the levels of pleasure and joy in your existence.

To permanently eliminate your negative beliefs, adhere to the following fundamental principles.

Gain control over your system of beliefs.

Understanding your personal perceptions, values and ideologies is the initial step in challenging negative beliefs. Once you have a firm grasp on these aspects, distinguish them following societal norms to determine whether your formed beliefs are acceptable to others or stem from your negativity.

Differentiating one's beliefs allows one to gain self-awareness and delve more profoundly into one's belief system. It facilitates the discernment of positive ideals from limiting beliefs, allowing the chance to rectify the former.

Develop the capacity to acknowledge and embrace your limiting beliefs.

Always, acceptance must precede the development of the ability to let go. Your current self is a reflection of all your beliefs. Your accomplishments and gains are the result of your life experiences, which may have contained different negative and positive developments, some of which may have been traumatic and contributed to the formation of negative beliefs.

Unavoidably, negative experiences will happen. They can cause one to fear for one's safety and convince one that the world is unsafe. These beliefs are established unconsciously; therefore, one must accept one's past and ultimately relinquish those negative memories to change them.

Release and liberate oneself from constraining beliefs.

You should relinquish all negative beliefs once you have acknowledged and accepted them. Eliminating oneself from all negative thoughts and emotions can induce joy and revitalization.

An enormous burden appears to have been lifted from one's shoulders. The sight of light at the end of the tunnel represents optimism and a chance to effect substantial transformation.

Develop constructive beliefs and diligently strive to improve them.

Now is the time to construct a new belief system that leads to success, happiness and contentment if you wish to effect change. This recently developed conviction will be a source of motivation and hope in your quest to improve yourself.

Developing new positive beliefs will empower you to pursue your goals with increased motivation and assurance. Nothing can prevent you from achieving your goals. Your triumph over negative beliefs will fill you with satisfaction and gratitude; all that is required is acknowledging and transforming them into positive ones.

There are different strategies available for overcoming and changing limiting beliefs. One can employ daily affirmations to overcome negativity and implant it into one's subconscious. Utilizing a combination of positive affirmations, self-hypnosis and visualization is among the most effective methods for transforming negative beliefs into assets.

WHAT IS RESTRICTING YOUR PROGRESS?

On the list of the ten most prevalent obstacles encountered by individuals, fears, limiting beliefs and dwelling on the past are among the most prevalent. Furthermore, you can eliminate all three if you truly desire to improve your life. Although this may be easier said than done, consider the following: "Why is it so effortless to complain about the state of affairs and continue living as you do?"

The word comfort is evoked. At the same time, there may be times when you desire and wish to change certain circumstances in your life. The comfort and familiarity of being in your comfort zone is considerably less intimidating than confronting your fears. Furthermore, relinquishing the past is tantamount to forfeiting one's life, given that one lives it therein—in the past.

Your limiting beliefs have always determined your self-perception and daily activities, as you have chosen to accept them without questioning their validity. In addition, if you believe them, limiting beliefs deprive you of everything you desire to experience and add nothing to your life. They are invisible barriers that confine you to your convictions.

How do you eliminate the three most significant obstacles that impede your progress?

The most effective way to overcome one's anxieties is to traverse them. Do the very thing that terrifies you! Remind them that you are now in charge and have a new strategy each time your concerns come true. Upon dissection, one will probably ascertain that they were fabricated.

Similar to how you imagined the boogie man to be genuine when you were a child, many fears also originate in your mind. You will discover that they have less influence over you than you initially believed. If you don't conquer your anxieties, they will.

Subsequently, arrange your limiting beliefs on the table. Proceed to analyze them by posing a series of critical inquiries to yourself, including but not limited to: Does this assertion hold? Are your statements entirely factual? What are the consequences of maintaining this conviction?

Who else would I be if not for this thought?

What would the absence of this thought entail for my existence be like?

Could the opposite belief be true too? Many other questions can dig into what a belief is based on.

Then swap the outdated negative belief for a fresh, helpful one. When the old thought tries coming back, return to the new belief - you're retraining your subconscious mind.

Furthermore, how does one cease to exist in the past?

Put an immediate end to it! Although I am joking, I am not. It would be best if you initially recognized that the past exists only in your mind. It has passed, become obsolete and is no longer a reality; it is the past and it exists solely because you continue to contemplate it. The act of reliving it through habitual thought sustains its existence. Presently, this very instant is what is real.

By failing to embrace the present, one will continue to enslave oneself by dwelling on the past and experiencing suffering. Acceptance entails confronting the truth. When one accepts reality, they cease to resist it, thereby liberating themselves from the burdens and experiences of the past.

You now understand the factor impeding your progress toward living your desired life. There may be additional challenges, but these are the major three. Once you overcome these obstacles, you can begin living the existence you've always desired, superior on every level. Do the thing you believe you are incapable of doing; it will be worthwhile!

Doubts, concerns and fears

These three limiting beliefs have the potential to impede one's progress. They have the potential to impact us at any given moment negatively. These pernicious thoughts decide to sneak into your mind, draw up a chair and throw a party the day after you're doing well. Even more so, they were not invited!

They can disrupt one's day, introduce additional tension and anxiety (as if that weren't enough), provoke introspection regarding one's actions and motivations, and dampen enthusiasm. They disregard the signs that read "No Trespassing" and destroy your mental property. How, then can they be expelled from one's mind?

It would help if you mobilized the L.B.B. (Belief, Faith and Trust) as Limiting Belief Busters. A warrant is issued for their apprehension and they are subsequently incarcerated.

Otherwise, you will be confined within your domain, helpless to apprehend them, as they will increase. You permitted their intrusion by permitting the watch officer to depart for vacation.

Concerns, anxieties and concerns acquire the force you attribute to them and nourish them by recognizing their presence, attentively considering their perspectives and relinquishing resistance as they assert themselves. One's mind is personal, and if something attempts to disrupt contentment, that person has every right to dismiss it.

These intruders have no chance against faith, trust and belief. Embrace them into your realm and they shall guide you in the right direction and safeguard your tranquility and harmony. Everything depends on what you allow in.

Everyone occasionally encounters fears, doubts and concerns that call on their door; however, the decision to acknowledge or disregard them is entirely within your control. Do you emphasize the items you wish to avoid at a buffet dinner? Alternatively, do you consider all the positive aspects that are possible?

Your limiting beliefs and thoughts are the same. You will become ailing and exhausted due to having a mind full of them if you concentrate on them. Instead, surround yourself with confidence, faith and trust that your divine source—whatever you may refer to as God, your Higher

Power or whatever—has your back and will furnish you with precisely what you require.

Constantly beset by worry, uncertainty and fear you will make no space in your life for the goodness that is knocking. Who then do you intend to invite to your party?

Changing Your Pessimistic Beliefs.

Our lives outcomes are determined by our beliefs regarding ourselves. You are nable to obtain your deepest desires in life because your beliefs have prevented you from reaching that point. Certain convictions will empower you, while others will prove detrimental and have no impact.

Before anything else, it is essential to determine which of your beliefs are the most empowering in your life. Which of your personal beliefs most significantly enables you to effectuate positive change?

Such convictions may include "I am deserving of good things," "I am humorous," "I am intelligent," and "I am worthy." A considerable number of them exist. Which ones do you currently have in your life?

At this moment, we must recognize our negative beliefs. Could you kindly list some of the negative beliefs that you hold? What are many factors that are impeding your progress?

For instance, "I am not intelligent" or "I am overweight." I dislike meeting new people, "That's just the way I am," "I am shy," "I am unable to attain wealth," and "I am unable to find a job that I am passionate about." All these prevalent negative and self-restrictive beliefs impede an individual from attaining their true desires.

Could you kindly list some of the beliefs that you hold? Please generate a minimum of three beliefs that are impeding your progress. Recognizing and appreciating the presence of positive beliefs is an essential initial step. We intend to place those in a more prominent position.

Conversely, we must take action in response to our negative beliefs. However, we can't simply eliminate the negative beliefs, as it is impossible to eliminate a belief. It must be replaced. One must substitute a pessimistic belief for one that is more empowering.

For instance, it is not sufficient to disregard the belief that "I am shy" and declare, "All right, I am now extroverted." That is most likely impractical. Your intellect will inform you, "Whoa, whoa, whoa, our acquaintance is non-existent."

You could say, "At this time, I experience anxiety when interacting with strangers; however, that is a characteristic I am capable of developing away from." It is not a characteristic to be timid. It is merely a behavior, essentially the result of experiencing anxiety when meeting a new individual.

Substituting the notion that "I am shy" with "I experience social anxiety; however, it is a trait that I can cultivate and improve" is a significantly more empowering perspective and will not elicit negative cognitive responses from you.

While confronting your negative beliefs, Engaging in this process will require diligence and consistent practice. Upon recording your newly formed convictions, affix them to a 3x5 card and bear it with you at all times. Read them regularly.

By gradually replacing your negative beliefs, you will eventually be able to manifest the life that you truly desire. One could envision yourself potentially becoming a high school motivational speaker in the future, imparting your message to the youth.

One of the principles elucidated in Manifesting through the Law of Attraction is that limiting beliefs often impede progress. Although this is true (and I will discuss some belief busters in a moment), I would like to emphasize that limiting beliefs can also serve a purpose in one's life.

Limiting beliefs are those that confine us to a specific domain. The fact that our box establishes the boundaries of the reality we perceive can be advantageous because it provides stability.

It provides assurance, for example, that our address and place of employment will remain unchanged from when we depart for work in the evening until we arrive back the following morning.

Also, it signifies that we can visit the grocery store to ensure that the items we seek are available. Thus, limiting beliefs contribute to the establishment of order in the world. Not that terrible, huh?

Difficulties arise when limiting beliefs prevent us from achieving our aspirations. For example, if your belief system holds that there are no available positions, then your job search may be somewhat constrained.

Notably, limiting beliefs don't constitute the complete truth. Instead, they constitute one's subjective interpretation of reality and upon reaching that realization, you will have already begun to surmount the obstacles they pose.

Okay, now for some dispellers of beliefs. Consider the following inquiries and observe whether you don't emerge with a marginally changed viewpoint:

Nothing is ever all or nothing; this way of thinking is extremely restrictive because it makes no allowances for exceptions. Consider the employment example that was provided earlier. For instance, is it true that NO ONE can find employment during a recession? I mean, truly, nobody?

Although this may be the current economic climate, it doesn't apply to all individuals globally. Therefore, it is not wholly or nothing if even a single individual manages to secure employment. It is also possible for you if it is possible for one individual. How does all-or-nothing thinking influence the formation of limiting beliefs?

Diverse cultures exhibit distinct customs. For instance, shaking hands to express salutation is customary in the United States. This practice is disapproved of in other nations and may even be met with disapproval. Who then is right?

Every one of us lives in a unique region of the globe. Because it is simple to assume that is how the world is everywhere, customs foster limiting beliefs. Which cultural presumptions are the sources of your restrictive convictions?

Generally, everything begins somewhere and for a practical purpose. Which limiting beliefs continue to persist because the situation has consistently remained unchanged?

"I can't." These two uncomplicated words likely contribute more than anything to forming limiting beliefs.

How does one determine that they can't?

Did you attempt?

Have you conducted an adequate inquiry into the potential options?

Have you ever engaged in self-deprecating thoughts before taking the initial action?

Dreams are stifled by the near-impenetrable barrier that I can't overcome. Which of your aspirations have been dashed due to your use of the phrase "I can't"?

Recognizing limiting beliefs for what they truly are will significantly enhance their ability to attract desired outcomes. This is because, upon recognizing the fallacy, one possesses the agency to determine whether or not to persist in accepting it. You better believe it!

STRATEGIES FOR CONQUERING NEGATIVE SELF-TALK

"Make lemonade when life gives you lemons" is an adage that conveys the following: "How do you cope with a bad day?" Do you self-blame or vent your frustrations in response to adversity, believing you are doomed to fail?

Any amount of negative self-talk has the potential to become ingrained. Embrace a positive outlook on life and permanently eliminate negative self-talk by following these suggestions:

Document your thoughts in writing.

Most thoughts originate from the subconscious mind, which can be challenging. With practice, however, you can effectively manage your "inner dialogues" by transcribing them to paper. Initially, it might be mentally taxing, particularly if writing is not your forte but it will undoubtedly stimulate your thoughts and you will adore it.

Observe your speech.

Reread them after you've written them down and consider whether your self-talk is assisting you in coping with the negative situation. To facilitate the procedure, contemplate the subsequent inquiries:

- What emotions does your self-talk evoke?
- Do you have any evidence to support your negative criticisms against yourself?
- How does it benefit you? Do they prove to be useful?

Perform an action.

After identifying the cause and intent of your self-talk, change your thinking and adopt a more optimistic perspective. As previously stated, even minor negative self-talk has the potential to develop into an undesirable habit.

Discuss your inner dialogue with others.

Seek solace in a family member or friend with whom you can share your thoughts. Not only will it alleviate your concerns but that individual may also offer a novel viewpoint on how you ought to approach challenges and mistakes.

Positively attract concepts

Has one experimented with the "positive way of thinking"? This technique is for counteracting negative beliefs with positive ones through positive, uplifting self-talk. Consider an individual who is experiencing difficulty reducing weight.

Rather than uttering the condemning thought, "My appearance is abhorrent and I will never be able to change my life as I desire," he examines himself in the mirror and resolves, "I am capable of achieving my goals of weight loss and lifestyle modification; I will start the process immediately!"

You, too, can change your perspective by speaking positive thoughts to yourself. Adopting a "positive way of thinking" as your mantra will attract contentment and positive energy.

Identify your pessimistic mentality.
Putting a silly moniker to your negative ego assists you in relaxing and attracting positive energy. An individual once resorted to self-deprecating remarks such as "useless," "boring," "dull," and "ugly." Consequently, he designates his interior critic as " Perfectionist."

Set aside a couple of minutes from social media.
According to studies, social media usage elevates self-criticism. Therefore, pause for a while and focus on your thoughts.

Accept your faults. Your mistakes will not diminish your humanity. At the very least, whenever you sense yourself reverting to a pessimistic outlook, remind yourself to find the positive in every circumstance.

Remember that your beliefs influence your behavior and the people in your vicinity; therefore, ensure that you attract only positive energy. Relax, take a deep breath and allow your courageous nature to prevail.

A recent survey of over two million of my clients revealed that more than fifty percent acknowledged struggling with negative self-talk. Despite having a brilliant concept, you may defeat yourself before starting. Do you ever feel as though you are reasoning yourself out of success?

The Henry Ford quote, "In either case, you are correct, whether you believe you can or can't accomplish it" is one of my favorites. The mind is a potent indicator of our success; if we succumb to its influence, we will be dissuaded from undertaking challenging or uncomfortable endeavors, impeding our development and deviating from success.

Perhaps you begin to establish goals for yourself but then have persistent doubts that you cannot accomplish the task or lack the qualifications to see it through.Regardless of whether you have encountered either circumstance, you must modify your approach toward your inner critic; indeed, everyone has one.

Rather than succumbing to this rudimentary defense mechanism, one can employ positive self-talk to counteract the negative aspects and conquer most apprehensive thoughts; this knowledge is invaluable.

Developing and Maintaining Goals through Positive Self-Talk

When individuals establish goals for themselves, they are often overcome with self-doubt and self-defeating thoughts that impede their progress before commencing the endeavor.

When you continually talk yourself out of achieving success, it can be challenging to maximize your life. Having these notions persistently trouble you can be discouraging and aggravating. Quite a few of us are unaware that we possess them! We only know we lack the confidence to adhere to our strategies and accomplish our goals.

Conversely, an alternative approach exists!

Implementing positive self-talk can be a highly effective strategy for establishing and maintaining goals, even for those who have not yet achieved such success. In this process, you determine which objective is most significant to you and devise the logistical details necessary to achieve that objective.

You will counteract the negative pressure with affirmations that validate your accomplishments whenever self-doubt begins to set in. It is evident from the fact that you are reading this chapter that you are not a failure and are not a quitter; therefore, begin to have faith in yourself!

How to Reprogram Your Mind

In essence, affirmations are positive statements that reprogram the mind to perceive only the positive. You can counter a self-defeating thought with a motivating statement the instant you have it.

Positive affirmations include the following: "I am deserving of tremendous success" and "By becoming a member of that group, I envision myself effecting change." Doing so can supplant negative thoughts with constructive ones that facilitate progress toward one's goals rather than deterring further from them.

Positive self-talk is surprisingly simple to incorporate into one's life. Perhaps you are oblivious to the gravity of the negative dialogue presently occupying your mind. However, as soon as you begin using positive self-talk, you will realize that you are sabotaging those goals the moment you set them.

Engaging in this procedure may enlighten you to the extent to which this internal dialogue has disrupted your existence. You'll feel hopeful that you can now set goals and surpass them.

By employing positive self-talk, one can effortlessly establish both immediate and long-term goals for oneself. Furthermore, by employing affirmations, you will have readily available resources to assist you in surpassing your previous limits. When did you consciously silence your inner critic and realize your decision was good?

One's outlook and personality are profoundly influenced by the thoughts and beliefs they express to themselves. The determining factor is not the events themselves but rather the individual's internal response to those events.

How will you converse with yourself influence your emotions, sentiments, and behavior? One will have greater control over all facets of life if one can cultivate a constructive and efficient method of self-talk.

Reflect for a moment on the following: Whenever you encounter a challenge in life, recall the words that crossed your mind. The word you choose to describe the situation is critical, as it will determine the tone and quality of your emotional existence.

Individuals who adopt a constructive and positive outlook, consistently searching for the positive aspects of every circumstance, are more likely to exhibit optimistic attitudes. Therefore, focus on your desire and divert your attention from what you fear or dislike.

Regrettably, people are inevitably confronted with obstacles and difficulties in their lives. However, you will become stronger if you view every difficulty as an opportunity to develop and find an effective solution.

Successful people typically face more obstacles than average people but how they respond to each one empowers them. Consequently, our success is contingent on how we navigate life.

What differentiates an optimist from a pessimist?

A setback or failure is perceived as transient by the optimist but permanent by the pessimist. Consider the following when confronted with a setback: "Will it impact you in a year?" If the answer is no, then proceed with your life. Therefore, inquire of yourself whether you lean towards pessimism or optimism.

Maintaining a positive perspective and attitude depends entirely on how you engage in regular self-talk. An inevitable response to any problem is transforming it from negative to positive. Why? Why not select the constructive thought since the subconscious can only store one thought at a time? Such action would be more constructive.

By maintaining congruence between your positive self-talk and mental imagery with your intended goals and goals, nothing can impede your path to achieving the success you so richly deserve.

By adhering to the adage "Success doesn't come to you; you must work towards it," I established this self-help website to inspire and motivate my online friends following my empowering voyage and striving for self-empowerment.

MANAGING REJECTION AND CRITICISM

In the Hans Christian Andersen story "The Ugly Duckling," brothers make fun of and reject a duckling that looks different from the others. This story is a great example of pain and rejection.

The baby duck was made fun of, left out of social groups, and looked down upon so badly that he saw himself through the eyes of those who made fun of him. He became more and more hateful toward himself because of this skewed view of things.

Depression often ensues from an inability to manage rejection; it can precipitate a cascade of emotional problems that negatively impact an individual's physical and mental health. Surmounting the psychological repercussions of rejection is likely among the most agonizing obstacles to surmount.

It can profoundly change an individual's perspective or manner of thinking about life. Rejection permeates various domains, including personal, social and professional spheres and instills within its victims a profound sense of being unloved, unappreciated and unvalued.

"Much of the time, fifty percent of the damage is caused by rejection, and the remaining fifty percent is our fault," says Guy Winch, who has a Ph.D. in clinical psychology from New York University and is a member of the American Psychological Association (APA). "We start with this high volume of negative self-talk and criticism that takes the rejection to another level," he claims.

What happens to an individual who feels rejected?

Rejection not only induces unwarranted anxiety and envy but also causes substantial harm to an individual's psychological health. Some adverse consequences associated with rejection include:

Formation of neural pathways associated with physical pain: According to neurological research, individuals who undergo rejection experience activation in the same brain regions stimulated during physical pain. This explains why the effects of rejection are comparable to physical suffering.

Decreased sense of belonging: Belonging to a similar group is an innate human desire; rejection undermines this desire and induces emotional distress. Reestablishing connections with a collective that fosters profound affinity is probable to alleviate the distress.

Anxiety escalation: Rejection is a primary catalyst for acts of violence among the youth demographic. In addition to exhibiting aggression towards others, such aggression possesses a high propensity to transform and result in a range of psychological disorders.

A decline in self-esteem: In certain instances, individuals may stigmatize themselves after experiencing rejection. Reflecting on one's shortcomings following a significant setback diminishes one's sense of self-worth and induces considerable emotional distress.

A decline in IQ: It is impossible to think rationally and make prudent decisions when distressed by a distressing rejection. The agony can be exacerbated by the mental debilitation caused by recalling the moments of rejection.

The recurrence of social pain is more distressing than physical pain: The brain's neural pathways may continue to react in the same way when one recalls a rejection incident that caused significant physical pain. Consequently, the same old emotions of despair and anxiety may resurface.

Managing the suffering that rejection causes

It is normal to experience jitteriness in response to rejection; however, many meditate on the disappointment for far too long. Regrettably, individuals who exhibit a heightened sensitivity to rejection must endure an immense cost for their desire to be accepted, even though many individuals endure rejection and the subsequent depression in secrecy, the consequences can be severe.

Embrace Your Individuality

In a society preoccupied with conformity and social comparison, embracing individuality and living life on one's terms is essential. It is critical to recognize that each individual is unique and that embracing one's differences will result in a more satisfying and joyful existence. The choice of contentment is at your discretion.

Operating from one's truthfulness and prioritizing self-determination is critical to achieve happiness and live authentically. Living your own life to discover inner peace and remain true to yourself is essential.

Self-Defining Your Identity.

Living one's own life and accepting individuality are fundamental components of existence. It is the only way to guarantee integrity and develop a purposeful existence.

Life is not a one-size-fits-all endeavor; therefore, attempting to conform to the predetermined life plan of another individual is fruitless and detrimental to one's sense of self-value.

By embracing your individuality, you can learn to trust yourself and make decisions consistent with your values and goals. Also, you will gain self-assurance and confidence in your identity as you realize you are leading your own life.

Exploring Individual Fulfillment.

One can become readily absorbed in the concerns and problems of others. The highlight videos on social media possess the capacity to fabricate the perception that each person lives a successful and cheerful life.

Nevertheless, it is essential to remember that comparison diminishes delight. One must acknowledge and value their distinct attributes to achieve personal fulfillment and contentment.

As life is an individual's journey, it is essential to focus on experiencing one's own life rather than observing the experiences of others. Individuals can forge a distinctive trajectory by assuming responsibility for one's narrative, decisions, and unabashed authenticity. Possibilities are virtually limitless when one establishes one's standards.

You can define success and devise a strategy to achieve it. After deciding to live your own life and embrace your true self, you may uncover a distinct sense of satisfaction and happiness that is uniquely yours.

Developing Self-Esteem and Self-Confidence.

Recognizing and accepting one's individuality is fundamental to developing self-assurance and self-worth. Living authentically and refraining from comparing yourself to others can foster a sense of self-assurance.

Self-comparisons make it easy to feel inadequate in the eyes of others. However, self-esteem can be developed nonetheless if one takes the time to recognize and value their distinctive qualities and strengths. Recognizing and valuing one's individuality will enable one to recognize the worth and unique contributions that one's life possesses.

This practice will aid you in focusing on improving yourself rather than engaging in self-comparisons that induce feelings of inadequacy. Self-directed individuals can make decisions that align with their personal preferences and further their goals, instead of conforming to external pressures.

Creating Your Options and Decisions.

Individual agency and the ability to make decisions are essential elements of being human. Acknowledging and embracing one's unique personality and preferences is paramount.

By doing so, one can lead a life consistent with their authentic self-perception and personal principles, disregarding the views and concerns of others. Also, it enables you to make decisions that are in your best interest without fear of criticism or disappointment.

Devoting time to verifying that the decisions and choices one executes will ultimately yield favorable outcomes for one's life and inspire a sense of pride is a worthwhile endeavor. Gaining self-assurance in one's inclinations and reestablishing agency over one's life via decision-making constitutes a powerful result.

Embracing Responsibility and Accountability.

It is widely acknowledged that life can occasionally present challenges, especially when an individual feels compelled to live another person's life. Conversely, by embracing one's uniqueness, one bestows oneself the liberty to lead an authentically personal existence.

Instead of constantly relying on the desires and expectations of others to justify your decisions, you can exercise autonomy by choosing options that align with your gratification and are in your best interest.

Adopting personal responsibility and accountability allows individuals to exert control over their lives, thereby facilitating the development of a gratifying existence. Embracing one's unique identity grants individuals the agency to take accountability for their lives and make personally meaningful and gratifying choices.

Engaging in this activity may lead to a more fulfilling life and provide opportunities for discovery that may have otherwise evaded your attention. Therefore, assume responsibility and accountability for your life and embrace your uniqueness. It is never obligatory to live the existence of another individual, as one has every right to their existence.

Construction of Your Influence and Legacies.

Why not utilize individuals' unique capabilities, ambitions and passions to create a lasting impression and heritage? Recognizing and appreciating one's unique qualities is essential in embodying one's existence.

It is imprudent to conform to the expectations of others, given the transient nature of life. Individuals bear the onus of shaping their destinies and constructing meaningful and purposeful lives. One can potentially shape the trajectory of history and make a lasting impact on society through accepting and celebrating one's individuality.

Engaging in this endeavor will impact individuals in your immediate vicinity and testify to your dedication to this pursuit. By embracing one's uniqueness, one can freely express oneself without fear of criticism or evaluation and direct one's interests and capabilities toward developing an enduring heritage.

Developing Resilience and Adaptability.

It is imperative to acknowledge and cherish one's unique qualities and conduct one's life according to one's volition. Having a healthy sense of self-assurance and being one's genuine self enhances the probability of mustering the resilience and power required to confront the challenges and adaptations that arise throughout one's life.

Regardless of the obstacles that may emerge, preserving one's integrity and having unwavering faith in one's principles and convictions can aid in preserving composure in challenging situations.

Developing adaptability and resilience amid challenges is contingent upon this. By living life on your terms, you can also develop the ability to trust your intuition and make prudent choices. Your unique perspective and individuality may aid you in developing greater resilience and adaptability.

Overcoming Anxiety Regarding Rejection and Judgment.

Each individual is influenced by their own beliefs, emotions and life experiences. We must acknowledge our uniqueness and conduct ourselves in alignment with our truth.

When we live our own lives and are at ease in our skin, we can have confidence in ourselves and not fear the judgment or rejection of others because we are certain that our identities are genuine.

One who is secure in their identity is confident that others will acknowledge and appreciate them for who they truly are. One must overcome the fear of criticism and rejection by acknowledging and embracing one's uniqueness while living one's life.

Developing Sincere Relationships.

Real relationships require accepting yourself and staying true to who you are. Living authentically makes people see your value and trustworthiness. It also makes you more open to deeper bonds over surface-level ones.

When you're real, others tend to overlook quirks and flaws more. Authenticity fosters understanding and acceptance.

Also, being genuine motivates people around you to do the same. Staying aligned with your core values shows integrity that brings out the realness in others too.

So allowing yourself and others to embrace uniqueness is key for authentic connections to thrive.

Living a Purposeful and Meaningful Life.

Reaching your full potential involves loving what makes you different and living life on your own terms. To feel your life matters, take charge of it with purposeful choices. Discovering your true self gives you power to follow dreams, gain skills, and expand.

Also, you can increase your self-awareness by learning what makes you special and how to utilize those qualities to your advantage. One can attain greater satisfaction and meaning by leading an authentic life following one's core values, aspirations and goals.

Rather than yielding to the expectations of others, you will be able to make decisions consistent with your true self when you assume responsibility for your life. Therefore, embrace your uniqueness, don't fear being distinct and live your life with intention.

EMBRACE AFFIRMATIONS OF SELF-CONFIDENCE

The way we speak to ourselves has a profound impact on our self-esteem and self-confidence. This internal dialogue, often referred to as "self-talk," is within our control, even if we don't always realize it.

Negative self-talk, such as putting ourselves down or dwelling on our mistakes, can significantly undermine our self-worth. It's important to recognize these patterns of negative thinking and actively challenge them.

Instead of focusing on our shortcomings, we should cultivate a more positive self-talk. This involves affirming our strengths, acknowledging our accomplishments, and expressing gratitude for the good things in our lives.

It's also crucial to be honest with ourselves and avoid denying our true feelings or pretending to be someone we're not. False affirmations can be counterproductive, as they can lead to a sense of inauthenticity and further erode our self-confidence.

By embracing our true selves and focusing on our positive qualities, we can gradually reprogram our self-talk and build a more confident and self-assured mindset.

For instance, if you tend to shy away from social interactions due to your introverted nature, instead of telling yourself you should be more outgoing, focus on the strengths and advantages of your introverted personality.

Acknowledge your unique strengths, such as your ability to listen attentively, your insightful observations, and your deep thoughts. Remind yourself that being introverted doesn't mean you're any less interesting or valuable.

Embrace your authentic self and appreciate the gifts that your introversion brings to the world. By reframing your self-talk in a positive light, you can cultivate a more confident and self-assured mindset.

Acknowledge that each personality type is distinct and not superior to the others. One possible mental image is the following:

"That is Alex; he is outgoing and has blonde hair; he enjoys public speaking; I, too, am myself; I have brown hair; I am sociable and enjoy getting to know people on a deeper level; and I enjoy sharing my values with them; in any case, through your daily self-confidence affirmations, you want to emphasize that your qualities are equally valuable."

It is often a waste of time and, more significantly, prevents you from enjoying yourself and living a satisfying life. Also, it inhibits your creative energy.

Does self-doubt influence decision-making and stifle your enthusiasm and motivation to take action? Approximately what portion of your day is consumed by this superfluous negative emotion? However, were you aware that self-doubt can be deactivated effortlessly, swiftly and permanently, restoring your life? "How do you accomplish that?" you inquire.

Self-doubt is among the most harmful negative emotional states ever identified. If that seems exaggerated, allow me to explain my stance.

Converting Doubt Into Confidence

Self-doubt is an obstacle to one's creative potential and overall strength. In other terms, it conveys the following message:

- You lack the qualities necessary for success.
- Your efforts are inevitably doomed to fail.
- You are insufficient and deficient.
- You are insufficiently intelligent.
- You have failed.
- You have a deficiency.
- You have no utility.
- Success will never be yours and so forth.

Upon accepting such "lies" about oneself, an individual is immediately overcome with helplessness, despair, immobility, and lack of motivation, rendering them more likely to surrender. What am I giving up on exactly?

Essentially, it is giving up on existence. In essence, self-doubt is the primary cause of one's decision to surrender to death and cease living (yes, "seducing" is an appropriate term, as one does possess agency in this matter). In other words, allowing self-doubt to reside within oneself constitutes a suicidal covenant.

Consequently, how does one confront this hazardous entity?

To effectively and permanently eliminate self-doubt from one's mind and body, it is imperative to acknowledge and confront the subconscious beliefs that pertain to the beneficial nature of this detrimental emotion.

Indeed, many individuals unknowingly hold the belief that self-doubt serves a purpose for them. This is how many of you feel. One example is the belief held by some individuals that self-doubt is a protective mechanism against impulsive decision-making, functioning as a vital and practical self-regulatory mechanism.

Following this line of reasoning logically would lead one to conclude that self-doubt contributes to an individual's sense of safety, security, tranquility and serenity and their capacity to make lucid and focused decisions that ultimately enhance their quality of life.

If that seems peculiar to you, it is precisely because the logic is naturally flawed. Determine whether or not you can ascertain the reason. Self-awareness of this deficiency indicates that the process of eliminating self-doubt has started.

STRATEGIES AND METHODS FOR ENHANCING SELF-ESTEEM

Generally, individuals are perplexed as to what it means to have self-esteem. Simply put, self-esteem is recognizing and appreciating one's entire being, including all one's flaws and shortcomings.

It would appear that various cultures struggle with self-esteem to a lesser extent than the United States. Perhaps as an outcome of the pressures we experience, we tend to prioritize materialistic measures of self-esteem.

Individuals who have intelligent and healthy self-esteem are willing to accept themselves as they truly are. They recognize their worth and are proud of their abilities and achievements. Furthermore, they validate the bestowal of nature.

1. Conduct a self-assessment inventory.

Obtain some paper. Construct a line through its center. Ten of the following should be listed: "Strengths" on the right-hand side and "Weaknesses" on the left wing. Yes, 10. Even though this may appear to be a significant portion of your strengths if you have low self-esteem, make every effort to identify all ten.

This is your Inventory of Self-Esteem. It assists you in identifying all the things you have already told yourself about the proportion at which you suck, in addition to revealing that there are some things at which you don't suck. One may be able to prepare for the modification of many vulnerabilities if they are addressed individually over a month or even a year.

Remember that the Roman Empire did not get constructed overnight. Things are not changed within a brief period. Therefore, avoid establishing an unrealistic expectation that you will effortlessly make a change within a week.

2. Establish Practical Expectations.

Our self-esteem will never be destroyed by setting elusive standards. Occasionally, our expectations are considerably more modest and elusive. Reevaluate your expectations if you continue to be unsatisfied. Your self-esteem will be appreciative of your actions.

Also, this may aid in breaking the cycle of self-deprecating thoughts that reinforce one's low self-esteem. Establishing practical expectations for our lives can prevent us from failing to achieve an ideological objective.

3. Forget about attaining perfection and seize ownership of achievements and mistakes.

Absolute perfection is unattainable for any individual. Allow it to pass. I don't remember you making any progress toward becoming virtuous. It bothers me when you don't progress toward attaining the ideal physique, lifestyle, romantic partnership, offspring or domicile.

We are susceptible to the notion of perfection; consequently, we are prone to encountering an abundance of it in the media. Nevertheless, that is an artificial construction of society. It is non-existent. Rather, seize grasp of your achievements as you achieve them. Recognize the individual for what they truly are worth.

It is imperative to eliminate elements associated with mistakes committed in one's lifetime. It doesn't imply that you are a malicious individual; rather, it signifies that you, like everyone else, made a calculation mistake.

Mistakes are opportunities for growth and development; if we can only force ourselves to emerge from the misery and negative self-dialogue that we tend to dwell in, then we can examine the situation through the eyes of another individual.

4. Investigate Oneself.

Beyond the realm of personal assets and weaknesses, it encompasses much more. Furthermore, expose yourself to novel experiences, fresh perspectives, opportunities, ideas, endeavors and companionships.

Occasionally, when our self-esteem has taken a significant blow and we feel extremely low, we tend to believe that we have nothing to offer the world or others.

It can be learned through trial and error. However, individuals transform into the individuals they have always aspired to be through undertaking unusual endeavors and embracing risks.

How we perceive ourselves impacts our behavior and interactions with others. Even in jest, if you consistently criticize yourself, your subconscious may begin to believe what you say about yourself.

Consider the following straightforward example. If you tell yourself, "I lack self-confidence," you are telling the truth. Despite possessing the requisite knowledge and abilities, one will likely experience intimidation in most situations.

The peculiar thing is that individuals rarely attempt to accomplish something they don't believe they can do. Subsequently, a detrimental cycle ensues, intensifying their sense of worthlessness and undermining their self-assurance.

I enjoy conducting a brief exercise with many participates at this stage in which they compose a six-word label describing their life narrative. It is a fascinating and extraordinarily enlightening exercise. The following are examples:

* "Failed Lawyer finds Motherhood spectacularly fulfilling."

* "Left a Legacy. Leaving a Legacy"

* "Dawdled through my twenties. Now flying"

* "Tired of struggling, have no choice"

The first three convey that individuals are embarking on a journey; they anticipate their destination with anticipation. The first demonstrates that while she once felt like a failure, she now derives immense pleasure from being a mother.

Her career is no longer a label she bears because it is no longer significant. The final instance is among the most disheartening I have ever encountered. That is not merely a designation; it is akin to donning a lead coat. It is a prime example of how self-perception can significantly influence daily existence.

We all face obstacles at some point in our lives and I don't wish to minimize their gravity; they are genuine and often difficult. However, notwithstanding the situation, we always make a decision. That decision determines how we perceive ourselves concerning the situation.

After a period of collaboration, this mother rewrote her label. "Seeing the light, work in progress" was the inscription. Despite its candidness, the appraisal is nevertheless imbued with optimism. To return to you, the following are guidelines for determining which labels you do and whether they require replacement.

Spend some time creating a personalized label using a notepad. Remind yourself to limit yourself to six syllables. It ought to reflect your life and your emotions toward it.

* Subsequently, repeat the label to oneself and inquire about one's emotional response. Would you be pleased to inform family and acquaintances about your label? Is it the type of person who elicits a sparkle in your eye and a smile? Conversely, does it induce an urge for you to shed tears?

If your current label diminishes your spirits, you will endeavor to develop a fresh and more optimistic label. We are both aware that irrespective of one's outlook on life, extraordinary abilities and talents may lurk beneath the surface. We intend to utilize them to assist you in living a more energized and vital existence.

* Remember that your label reflects your self-perception and defines your conduct. To cultivate an atmosphere of optimism and hope, diligently strive towards refining it until it becomes an article of clothing that inspires pride.

A person with low self-esteem has a pessimistic outlook on life, contributing to despair and hopelessness. It appears that everything you see and do is challenging. Conversely, one who possesses a high sense of self-esteem perceives the world in an exceptionally positive light. You exude positivity in all you do and observe and others share your high regard for yourself.

The Roots of Low Self-Esteem

Developing either high or low self-esteem is possible with practice but we don't wish for the latter to happen. Poor self-esteem may have a physical origin. Unattractiveness happens when an individual is excessively thin or obese.

It can also manifest mentally, such as when you are overly emotional, believe you are unintelligent, inadequate or lack sufficient knowledge. These are only a few instances in which individuals may experience low self-esteem.

Now that we know the factors contributing to low self-esteem, we must take action to change that which undermines our confidence.

There are many methods by which one can cultivate one's self-esteem. Possibly the most important step is to compile an inventory of your strengths and abilities. This serves as a reminder of the many tasks that require attention. Concentrate and amplify using all of your strengths. Also, you do not need to consider your shortcomings; all you desire in life is positivity.

One must also be mindful of their self-talk.

Your objective is to replace negative self-talk with positive beliefs. A positive statement regarding oneself constitutes a positive affirmation.

Implement them into a meditation regimen. A few positive affirmations should cross your mind, including "I am strong," "I will succeed," and "I can." Always keep in mind that you should never consider the negative.

Also, self-nurturing is vital for enhancing self-esteem. Begin by attending to your physical health by eating well, maintaining a healthy weight, exercising regularly and getting sufficient sleep (neither too much nor too little). Remember that one must feel good to appear good. This will increase your sense of self-assurance.

Self-esteem can ultimately be enhanced by reading literature. Indeed, perusing self-help books can be of great assistance. You are capable of acquiring diverse knowledge. However, reading books on self-improvement and self-esteem is not strictly necessary; one can benefit from perusing motivational and inspirational literature to foster an optimistic outlook on life.

UNDERSTANDING THE POWER OF OPTIMISM

A good outlook on life can have a significant impact on our thoughts and actions. When we believe in ourselves and our ability to achieve our goals, we are more likely to pursue them with determination and perseverance. This positive attitude can also attract others to us, who can provide us with support and encouragement.

Our thoughts are a form of energy that can shape our reality. By focusing on positive thoughts, we can attract positive experiences into our lives. This belief is consistent with the idea that we are all creators, and that our thoughts have the power to manifest our desires.

The evidence suggests that there is some truth to this belief. Studies have shown that people who have a positive outlook on life are more likely to be successful in their careers and relationships. They are also less likely to suffer from stress, anxiety, and depression.

If you are looking to improve your life, one of the best things you can do is to cultivate a positive attitude. This may not be easy at first, but it is definitely worth the effort. By believing in yourself and your ability to achieve your goals, you can create a life that is full of happiness and success.

If we believe that the universe functions as a higher entity, then we also hold the conviction that our positive thoughts generate energy within ourselves. This energy is capable of generating virtually anything. Some believe genuine smiles are contagious and everyone should be beaming. For some of us, happiness can be felt simply by witnessing the delight or smile of another individual.

While some individuals are fortunate, others struggle with pessimism and find little cause for happiness; sometimes, they even lament that others are as sad or dissatisfied as they are.

It is not difficult to comprehend how a positive outlook and thoughts could enhance the quality of our existence. Success requires the adoption of a positive outlook and the elimination of all negative beliefs.

Love, kindness, fortitude and joy are familiar to us and others; they are considered noble virtues. However, such occurrences don't happen spontaneously. Emotions and experiences require commitment, focus, optimism and mental fortitude.

It often requires an effort to adore the individuals we are obligated to. It can be difficult to exhibit courage or kindness. While instant solace may be found in the alternatives, exhibiting hostility and fear will not contribute to our success.

Our preoccupation with others, specifically their opinions of us, often prevents us from acknowledging our thoughts and emotions regarding the situation. While we are in motion, it is not to impress ourselves but to impress others.

- Your Beliefs form Your Environment.
- Advance Health
- Effect On The Constitution
- Influence And Mold The Course Of Events.
- Initiate The Process Of Creation.
- Impact on Individuals' Physiology And Psychology
- Achieve Prosperity

An Account of Optimism

Once upon a time, a thief was apprehended while attempting to take the King's Horse in a vast kingdom. For his offense, he was brought before the King to receive punishment. The king peers down upon the petty thief and requests, "Give me one reason why I shouldn't immediately amputate your head."

The thief gazes at the monarch and states, "Long live the King. You have all the power to do as you wish, Majesty. But I just wanted to let you know I have a unique gift. If you give me one year, I can teach your horse to fly."

The King found this man's assertion amusing. After careful deliberation, he ordered that this individual be confined for a year while being granted the opportunity to interact with his preferred equine companion. If he fails to achieve success within a year, he will be executed by hanging.

The thief was transported to the correctional facility, where the prison officer discovered the thief's delight while locking him up. The prison warden asked him," What was the point of that? You are not going to make that horse fly. You are going to be killed after one year anyway."

The prisoner responded with a grin and said, "The King, I or the Horse could all pass away within a year. Furthermore, who knows, the Horse might even master flight!"

A sense of optimism. Is it Practical?

I have always perceived optimism as a mechanism employed by cowards incapable of accepting the harsh realities of existence. However, this brief anecdote, which you may have previously encountered, exemplifies optimism's most advantageous manifestation. Here, the criminal employs optimism for two purposes.

Initially, when apprehended and certain to die for his transgression, he employs optimism to fortify himself against certain death. He never experiences depression or begs for pardon.

Conversely, he employs a small amount of deceitful reasoning to grant himself one final opportunity to preserve his life. Undoubtedly, every one of us is considerably more intelligent than this criminal.

However, what use is all the intellect in the world if it is useless when the moment comes when your life is at stake? We all succumb to pressure and cannot think clearly when confronted with significant challenges (which are likely minor compared to the one this criminal was confronting) due to our lack of optimism that prevents us from giving ourselves that final opportunity.

Furthermore, after addressing the immediate issue and allowing sufficient time to resolve it, he refrains from contemplating how he will accomplish the seemingly impossible challenge of teaching the horse to soar.

On the contrary, he maintains an optimistic outlook on the future by contemplating potential favorable outcomes, notwithstanding their improbable occurrence. Either I will be able to do something to save his life or he will be able to spend his final days in comfort and joy.

Untold is the ultimate fate of the criminal in this narrative. Thus, the story's conclusion is not conventional. Regrettably, if one believes that the narrative culminates in the thief's apprehension for his transgression, one no longer comprehends the crux of the story.

Most significant challenges encountered throughout our lifetimes are accompanied by more negative than positive outcomes. Now, by fixating on the many negative possibilities, we are not bolstering our case; in fact, we may be jeopardizing the few opportunities that appear to be impossible. Although that is not our intention, we often act that way.

Applying Optimism to One's Life

Therefore, the next time you encounter an impossible problem, adopt an optimistic stance and grant the impossible a greater chance at success than the problem itself. "In one year the King may die, I may die or the Horse may die. Moreover, who knows if the Horse may learn to fly!". Affirm this to yourself and your predicament will immediately appear somewhat more manageable.

Likely, many individuals in your vicinity have already informed you of the mind's immense power. What you believe typically transpires due to the subconscious unconsciously guiding us along that path in contemplation of our most profound thoughts.

For example, in basketball, persistently justifying one's inability to aim increases the likelihood of failing to deliver the ball to the rim. Undeniably, one can accomplish anything they set their mind to.

Many of us believe that if we can physically surmount the sensations our bodies are experiencing through our thoughts, we can do the same.

This is because individuals become more optimistic about their recovery efforts. As a consequence, the body progressively recovers as well. If you continue to believe that your illness will last eternally, you will be resistant to taking medications and treatments. That will only serve to exacerbate the situation.

The same holds about prosperity. Achieving success requires diligence and the ability to envision oneself accomplishing one's life's goals. "Success is achieved through laborious effort and 10% inspiration," as the adage goes.

Regardless of your endeavors, you must be able to envision yourself accomplishing your life goals, as your level of success is limited only by your imagination. Have faith in your ability to accomplish a goal and you will certainly succeed.

A paradigmatic dichotomy exists between optimistic individuals and those who are pessimistic. Optimistic individuals maintain a positive outlook and are certain that all will be well in the grand scheme.

They maintain that it is possible to accomplish any goal with diligence and perseverance, notwithstanding the challenges that may arise. They perceive challenges not as barriers but as opportunities for advancement via ladders and bridges.

On the contrary, the pessimists bear the burden of the world.

They hold the conviction that despite their utmost efforts, they will perpetually be condemned and unable to realize their aspirations. While occasionally acknowledging the negative aspects of life is acceptable, it is detrimental to allow oneself to become entirely engulfed in them.

A negative attitude toward something causes one to lose motivation and desire to do that action. Becoming pessimistic regarding one's future will inevitably result in losing optimism for that very future. Such is how the intellect functions. Your perspective on life will influence your behavior.

The mind is extremely potent due to its instantaneous ability to change the future. It can transform something negative or positive, depending on your perspective.

Consequently, it is critical that you continually reprogram your perspective whenever you become excessively pessimistic. Be optimistic and periodically perform positive affirmations.

Throughout my entire life, I have been characterized as an optimist. This is a term that I deeply appreciate and support. When an individual refers to me as an optimist, I experience a profound sense of being acknowledged and comprehended.

I am confident that my consistent manner of behaving in the world aligns perfectly with my desired experience; I am certain that my decisions reflect my true desires for myself. Yay me!

From that point forward, I observed a distinct quality and tone when individuals referred to me as an optimist a few years ago.

An abrupt onset of sneering, taunting and a form of mockery happened. The utterance "You're such an optimist" was met with exasperation and aggravation; optimism appeared to have acquired an undesirable connotation. Exactly what is that the matter of?

This "unexpected turn of favor," as I prefer to put it, is an issue that requires attention. I believe that optimism has been misconstrued somehow as a quality and a characteristic of humanity. It has been exalted to a certain extent; consequently, many individuals perceive optimists as detached from practicality. Therefore, we should clarify the situation.

Most would probably concur that optimists are, on average, upbeat individuals. An optimist is more concerned with devising solutions than dwelling on what is not functioning.

Difficulties are very real to an optimist but the optimist simultaneously seeks a solution to the difficulty that will either render it non-existent, advantageous or transform it from a challenge to an opportunity. Optimists are, on the whole, individuals who consider possibilities.

With that being stated, optimists are the subject of many fallacies. Many individuals believe that optimists are blind to problems. Contrary to that, optimists are unquestionably aware of problematic situations; they strive to find a means to bypass them.

There is a common perception that optimists cannot see the "negative side" of situations. You are once again mistaken. Even though an optimist can perceive the "negative aspects" of situations, personalities and other things, they also acknowledge the existence of positive aspects. Alternatively, an optimist possesses the ability to perceive alternative perspectives.

Occasionally, an optimistic perspective is portrayed as being detached from reality. Once more, this is untrue.

An individual who embraces optimism acknowledges that although they may be able to endure a problem-oriented reality, they stand to gain considerably more by adopting a more positive, optimistic outlook. It is indeed actuality; however, it is more agreeable and arguably more significantly fosters constructive and progressive progress rather than being predicated on issues.

Being an optimist means consistently assessing various options and perspectives, choosing the one that sparks the most energy and promise. The phrase "more often than not" is crucial because optimists, like everyone else, are flawed.

Despite their tendency to always look for the positive, they are not immune to occasional challenges. Optimism doesn't guarantee the absence of negative experiences.

Instead, optimism involves the belief that setbacks are temporary and can be overcome, usually through deliberate and purposeful decision-making.

Essentially, optimists are human too. They experience life's ups and downs, the struggles of being human, and the distress and anger that anyone might face. Their strength and resilience come from their ability to acknowledge obstacles, label them, and then choose the most empowering approach to deal with them.

The impact of your outlook on life and commitment to positive thinking extends to many people in your daily life. Everyday acquaintances like family members, coworkers, and neighbors are directly influenced by your disposition.

An optimist sees the best in the worst of circumstances, while a pessimist is presented with a half-empty glass. A pessimist fails to recognize opportunities amidst adversity, while an optimist does.

The choice of whether to be an optimist or a pessimist is a critical one that can significantly impact your path to success in life. Pessimism can easily sabotage any potential for professional or personal achievement.

Some claim, "I'm a natural pessimist." But pessimism, like many other emotions, is a learned behavior. An optimist will evaluate a situation and decide on the most favorable course of action to resolve it.

Difficulties are inevitable, and your goal is to move forward quickly. Optimistic people are positive because they believe that any challenge can be overcome swiftly.

Beware of cynicism, which is a poison that can hinder your success. Suspecting the success of others will only hinder your own efforts. Most successful people deserve their success.

Don't let negative thoughts dominate your life. Achieving success requires positive thinking and positive language. Self-affirming reinforcement will help you reach your desired level of success.

Recognize that life is full of obstacles. You must navigate around them or find an alternative route. A courageous individual, willing and able to persevere in the face of adversity, will be rewarded with a successful life.

NAVIGATING TOXIC RELATIONSHIPS AND NEGATIVE INDIVIDUALS

Much of your belief that you have no control over what happens in your lives is, to some degree, accurate. But your response to it is extremely significant. This response dictates whether you will proceed in a negative or positive direction.

Individuals who establish goals, generate enthusiasm and initiate a systematic progression towards their realization are more likely to experience greater happiness than those who don't.

The focus of negative individuals is deficiency and anxiety. To "build their ego," they disparage others or fixate on the negative aspects of the world. They take pleasure in highlighting the fallacies and deficiencies of others.

If you operate a home-based network marketing business, these unfavorable individuals probably expressed their disapproval. They wish to debunk the notion that it is a pyramid scheme or that you lack the necessary skills to succeed in the network marketing industry, much less any other business.

However, such negative remarks will be carried away by your intense determination if you are truly committed and certain of your ability to accomplish your goals.

What if they were to establish an objective upon which they could concentrate?

Concentrating On One's Goals Rather Than Others

Albert Einstein once advised, "If you desire happiness, attach it to a purpose rather than to people and material possessions." You may have observed that joyful individuals see the positive side of every situation and opportunity and are also extremely occupied and dedicated to an activity they are passionate about.

Content individuals consistently maintain a sense of purpose and engagement in pursuing their desired goals. They are not particularly mindful of their immediate surroundings. They truly begin an endeavor when they initiate it. They become completely oblivious to their surroundings since their actions hold immense significance.

Conversely, negative individuals are preoccupied with offering criticisms of others. The development of arrogance may impede their cognitive abilities. Typically, they lack goals to concentrate on. They are prompted to identify the initial mistake that you commit.

Due to their lack of progress, they require an outlet for criticism to ensure that those they know remain at their level. Upon observing individuals striving to improve themselves, they immediately launch into sarcasm and mockery.

Instead of concentrating on themselves, they were perpetually preoccupied with the actions of others. This certainly has the potential to diminish the pleasure of others. If your response is negative, reverse it. If you desire change and are negative, you must modify how you conduct yourself. How one thinks and moves is precisely what matters.

Whatever is exerting a detrimental influence on your life, you must eliminate it, including television, music, newspapers, books and even companions. You are required to locate those items and individuals that will increase your value.

Negative individuals are so intent on achieving results that they are willing to forego the process. Identifying and concentrating on the process and developing a strategic plan for the upcoming week, month, year or couple of years will undoubtedly transform your negative mindset and lead to favorable outcomes.

You will increasingly experience a sense of personal fulfillment in your existence. The more you experience that, the happier you will be and the more of that you desire will manifest in your life!!!

It is now your turn!

How do you maintain a positive attitude? How do you deal with negative individuals? Are you pessimistic and eager to change your outlook? Share and comment as you wish below.

Anticipated to start the perusing of them! In reality, only challenging moments exist and such experiences can have a direct effect on one's mental health. Concerning this, what steps can be taken? It seems to be devoid of any viable resolutions.

The following advice will be of assistance to you.

1. Define negative speech and conduct.

Consider a scenario in which you and your friend are conversing in agreement. That is an encouraging omen. When two or more individuals disagree or struggle with negative signs, one is met with criticism regarding all actions taken.

2. What indicators indicate negativity?

Negative conversations and arguments that are met with strong censure are extremely draining of your energy and positive disposition. It causes mental imbalance, anxiety, stress disorders, appetite loss, preoccupation with thoughts and an inability to concentrate and focus at work.

Individuals afflicted with negative behavior exhibit profound disappointments and a negligent demeanor. It also demonstrates that they are unconcerned with your remarks and are resolute in their counterarguments that they claim to be correct.

Individuals whom such individuals surround tend to maintain composure and eschew contentious discussions. Because they are aware that they will be apprehended if they attempt to defend their legitimate positions, this generates no positive energy.

3. What adverse consequences result from negative dialogues?

It demonstrates that they are in the right and you are in the wrong. One can't attain perfection when surrounded by negative individuals. They maintain an extremely firm grip on their arguments.

Your pronounced symptom is a fear of speaking and a preference for remaining silent.

- Negative individuals strive to establish their correctness and have various opinions to influence.
- The only purpose is to deplete your positive energies and force you to heed.
- Refute your claim
- They acquire vitality by compelling others to consider their arguments and perspectives.
- Compels you to await their verdicts and offer a discerning assessment of your actions.
- Extremely impulsive and lacks regard for others.

4. What course of action should be taken?

It would be best to exert tremendous effort to regain your positive attitude. Before you can accomplish this, you must avoid associating with negative individuals and attend to their conversations.

Have faith in your correctness and confidently speak regarding your views, opinions, works and statements. Having conclusive evidence and dependable judgments can sustain one's fortitude.

Never diminish, thereby creating an opportunity for negative individuals to exploit you.

Engage in the reading of literature that inspires optimism. Write down your thoughts and try to be positive in your work. Engage in different activities to occupy your mind when negative thoughts pursue you.

It may require time to recognize that negative individuals surround one. However, should you encounter any of the following indicators, it is opportune to cease your efforts and depart from the location permanently because it influences the development of one's personality, moods, psychology and decision-making ability.

One can ascertain one's place in society by distinguishing between constructive criticism and the expression of diverse perspectives.

An ordinary dialogue with an unfavorable individual may subject you to detrimental thoughts and render you a target. Paradoxically, it is impossible to resist. You can only maintain vigilance and motivation; you should not let others dictate your thoughts.

Have you ever interacted with a negative individual? Without a doubt, you may have! We encounter many individuals in our professional environments, including acquaintances, family members and others, who attempt to project their negative emotions onto us daily.

The sole determinant of maintaining protection is to discern the positive within the origin of negativity. On many occasions, nevertheless, it becomes exceedingly challenging to regulate.

Twelve suggestions for dealing with negativity and negative people are provided below. Included in these suggestions are strategies to prevent oneself from dwelling on negativity. Try them to maintain a positive attitude!

1. Avoid Arguments: You become an even greater fool by arguing with a negative individual. It will further impose negativity on you. It is best to change the subject or leave to avoid an argument. It is the finest solution to make the situation light.

2. Keep that Smile: Use this little curve on your face that works miracles. Keep pondering positive things in life and keep smiling. Also, make people around you beam as much as you can so that their negativity takes a rest. This will not only help overcome the effect of a negative person on you but will also enhance your confidence.

3. Value Your Thoughts: Give more importance to your thoughts than others' comments. Don't let anyone manipulate your thinking. It will help you acquire inner strength and will enhance confidence.

4. Go for Group Outings: Always hang out in groups to eliminate negative individual effects. This will allow you to have a limited conversation with the negative person and switching topics will be simpler.

5. Be Confident: Despite your best efforts, you may be drawn into a conversation with a negative individual. Avoid allowing them to lower your morale. Let your emotions and thoughts run wild and have confidence in your viewpoints.

6. Never React Aggressively: Never react aggressively to a negative person, even if provoked. Although negative remarks, sarcasm and the like may annoy you, please make an effort to disregard them and maintain a neutral stance. Attempt to leave the location during an impulsive moment and relax by walking around or listening to positive and constructive music.

7. Maintain your enthusiasm: Always be enthusiastic about your life and work. In many instances, actions speak louder than words. Consider negative remarks a challenge that you must overcome with your actions. Often embrace, smile or demonstrate affection towards such individuals to shield yourself from their negative energy.

8. Maintain a Positive Spirit: Regardless of how hard someone tries to bring negativity into your life, maintain a positive attitude and concentrate on your energy. Keep repeating good things to yourself so your positivity is not hampered.

9. Control Your Feelings: No matter how much feels to kick off a negative person, attempt to control your feelings and behave positively with them. Try to react to the negative person with a cool temperament and in a subdued voice.

10. Don't mind: Don't mind negativity from a negative source. When in conversation with a negative person, don't take anything personally and try to avoid any personal comments hurled at you.

11. Forgive Often: Forgive the person who does any negative to you. This will help you evolve emotionally and mentally. It will also help maintain excellent interpersonal relations with people around you. Moreover, will bring peace to your existence.

12. Ignore: If everything fails, attempt to ignore such people. Maintain a distance from them. It may sound harsh but it works.

Smile at them even though they are irritable. Although most individuals will likely respond negatively, you may be the only person who brings a smile to their faces that day. Please do whatever you can to potentially enhance their day. You will discover that your self-esteem is enhanced even further than if you had remained silent.

There is, without a doubt, at least one negative individual in your existence. They could be a close friend, coworker or even a member of your immediate family and it can be extremely difficult to know how to interact with negative individuals. This chapter contains extremely helpful and effective techniques and strategies for dealing with such individuals and negative situations.

It is initially critical to maintain your sense of self and identity. Because negative emotions are highly contagious, you mustn't allow others to bring you down with them. Constantly maintain the cheerful, extroverted and optimistic disposition that defines you.

Avoid forming too many negative judgments of others. They have assumed their current persona for different reasons, some of which may be perfectly reasonable but beyond your comprehension.

Try to be understanding and patient with those with whom you interact socially, reside or work. Individuals often emulate or duplicate the actions of those they associate with and as previously stated, you must refrain from imitating any negative conduct you are striving to address.

However, if you maintain a positive attitude in the face of any difficulty or circumstance, others may begin to do the same. A person who is typically pessimistic adopting your positive demeanor and persona can only benefit from this development.

A practical approach that can be implemented immediately is the practice of reminiscing. One strategy to assist a negative individual in overcoming a particularly degrading circumstance is to recall or draw parallels between the present situation and a happier, more optimistic past. This can occasionally provide individuals with an immediate positive outlook and resolution to a present dilemma.

Consider, for instance, a coworker who is extremely anxious about an impending interview with their supervisor. Although they might develop self-doubt and be extremely pessimistic about their abilities and how they will conduct themselves during the interview, it is possible to change their mind if you remind them of a time when they performed admirably for their employer, gave a persuasive presentation or achieved success in an interview.

Possibly one of the most productive strategies I have encountered, this can be implemented immediately with a friend, family member or coworker. Attempt it and determine for yourself how effective it is.

Despite appearances, removing oneself from a negative environment is an extremely difficult task. Certain individuals in your life are impeding your progress. Negative forces are present in your existence. I am virtually certain of it. We all have those individuals whose perspective is negative, regardless of our ideas.

It is straightforward that you eliminate those individuals from your existence. If there are certain individuals in your life whom you are unable to exclude, such as family members or close friends and they possess other admirable attributes, then you should, at the very least, refrain from involving them in your development endeavors.

Individuals of that nature will be the first to drag you down and will permit your progress to veer off course. An exemplary scenario would be if, despite your earnest efforts to cease smoking, you continued to associate with fellow smokers who regarded your efforts as frivolous.

They not only lack the desire to provide support but it is also in their self-interest to encourage you to resume smoking. They will not merely exhibit a lack of support; rather, they will proactively conspire against your efforts to cease smoking. They have motives to maintain your smoking habit. Consider that they will have one less justification for their negative behavior if you resign.

Whatever it may be, this holds in life. Negative individuals are motivated to prevent you from making progress. It is time to move on from those individuals or at the very least, to exclude them entirely from this voyage of self-improvement.

After eliminating the detrimental influences from one's life, effecting change will become an immeasurably simpler process. You will go from having a sideline of cheerleaders who support your every move to having a peanut gallery criticizing your every move if you can supplant the negative individuals with supportive ones.

Consider the distinction between the two situations. Envision substituting negative individuals in your life for a rotational schedule of motivational college lecturers. Impressive! That might be excessive, but having supportive individuals will do the trick.

DO YOU PRIORITIZE THE NEGATIVE COMMENTS OF YOUR PEERS OR YOUR DREAMS?

There are many justifications for the desire of many individuals to be their employer. We desire autonomy over decisions such as when to go on vacation and how much time to spend with our families.

Many of us opt to pursue this objective by establishing a home-based business. Owning a business can inspire a sense of self-importance and the belief that anything is possible.

Many of us become ecstatic that we immediately inform our closest family and friends about our new endeavor. Certain individuals receive assistance, while others become our team members, allowing us to collaborate closely.

It is an incredible experience to collaborate with individuals with whom we have shared personal connections; doing so transforms the work into something enjoyable and thought-provoking rather than a chore.

Conversely, certain individuals in high regard may also serve as "naysayers" in our lives. Operating under the assumption that they are illogical and rely solely on "hearsay" can present a formidable obstacle.

I say challenging because, rather than being an impediment, it puts your faith and perseverance concerning your aspirations to the test. When you cross these stepping stones, your conviction and the underlying spirit that motivates many of us to persevere will endure.

This is merely a test of your faith and as Napoleon Hill once said, "What the mind can conceive, it can accomplish." Therefore, you can accomplish anything you visualize in your mind. Consequently, why do so many of us receive negative feedback from our colleagues regarding our pursuits of dreams and goals?

One reason is that we don't wish to have our colleagues look down upon us. Also, we don't wish to lose the relationships in which we have developed such a strong attachment.

However, if they genuinely value your relationship, they should show you reverence for your actions, even if they disagree, correct? Maintaining connections with individuals you get along with and enjoy spending time with rather than those who don't share your interests is more important. Your satisfaction is entirely your responsibility.

Whenever you receive negative feedback, you may wish to consider whether elevating their criticism above the path you follow to accomplish your aspirations is more significant. This will ascertain the degree to which you regard your aspirations and fears. They will deviate from the intended path if you perceive them negatively.

HOW MIGHT IT BE POSSIBLE TO SURMOUNT THIS RESISTANCE?

It is important to remember that individuals who provide many negative comments were either accosted by an untrained and obnoxious industry professional or relied on hearsay and lacked knowledge regarding the business model.

Why, therefore, squander your time if they are unwilling to be enlightened and receptive to what you do? A greater likelihood exists that you could convert the ruler of the jungle to veganism.

It is one thing if your colleagues don't wish to follow your lead to advance; it is quite another to have those who wish to remain ignorant of the industry. If you lack supportive family and friends, the most effective course of action is to surround yourself with individuals who are also in the industry or, even better, to schedule more time to spend with those who are in the same business.

Undoubtedly, you will discover that your colleagues in network marketing are experiencing the same challenges you are. You can create synergy by mutually feeding off one another and providing substantial support for the operation.

You must surround yourself with the most exceptional individuals to accomplish your goals. Likewise, you must sever all connections with negative individuals who are presently a part of your existence. They are often preoccupied with dictating your way of life; to stop them, disconnect. Successful people cultivate a support system comprised of encouraging and positive individuals.

Warren Buffet, one of the wealthiest individuals globally, donated billions of dollars to Bill Gates, another of the world's richest, for placement in his charitable organization.

This is the optimal relationship to nurture and is one of the world's finest mastermind groups. Developing relationships with individuals with similar aspirations is essential to realizing one's goals.

Superman is the protagonist of a comic strip that describes and narrates his daily existence as a superhero and college student. Who do you currently perceive yourself to be? In reality, most of us aspire to be Superman and we would prefer to experience the gratification of saving lives and assisting others without the commotion.

Consequently, it is necessary to envision our lives as we would like them to be. One initiates the process of attaining one's aspirations by doing so.

As previously stated, surround yourself with individuals who share your values and observe their strategy. It would be best if you were dedicated to accomplishing your goals and focus on them throughout. Moments will pass when maintaining concentration proves difficult for whatever reason or circumstances may change. Your goals and strategy must shift in the same direction if this happens.

Tools to accomplish your goals are all around you; however, you will never notice them if you are unaware of your goals. Beginning with the most difficult step is always the first and worthwhile endeavors can require considerable time to accomplish.

If you begin to falter as you get started, remind yourself that you will reach your destination and ultimately realize your ambitions if you persevere and take even one more step forward.

"Some individuals achieve success only by putting others down" was the rumor. This holds regarding individuals who undermine your conviction. However, let us delve a little further. Why are these individuals so negative and critical?

This behavior is essentially a reflection of the individual. They enjoy pointing fingers at you as an explanation for your failure but they fail to notice that three fingers are pointing back at them.

Every negative word about you represents why that person has never achieved success and their lack of self-confidence. Others merely say it out of hatred, while others say it to shield you.

These individuals with negative qualities prefer to criticize others for pursuing their aspirations rather than taking the risk of pursuing their own. The good news is that many people are going through the same thing as you and you can certainly discover them to provide mutual support.

You have limited control over problematic individuals unless they are willing to change but you can surround yourself with more positive individuals who will encourage you to persevere. An advantageous aspect of the network marketing sector is the abundance of optimistic individuals devoted to their work. These individuals are the kind of companions you should spend time with.

By pursuing your dreams and taking calculated risks, you do the correct thing if you genuinely wish to live and escape mediocrity. Make an effort to maintain a positive attitude and concentration. "The Vortex" by Jerry and Esther Hick is a book that I wholeheartedly endorse.

Each individual possesses a tremendous amount of dormant energy. We were extremely attached to it when we were infants and toddlers but as the years passed, we became increasingly estranged from it. Reestablishing a connection with this potent positive force is the book's subject, which explains how to optimize one's life and accomplish desired goals.

DEVELOP A SPIRITUAL AND POSITIVE LIFESTYLE WITHOUT EVEN RUNNING AWAY FROM YOUR COMFORT ZONE

Spirituality is a way of life from which only a select few can benefit. Time and patience are required to incorporate spirituality into one's daily existence. Regardless of the perceived difficulty and complexity, it is possible to incorporate a greater spiritual dimension into one's existence without compromising comfort.

Understanding one's inner self doesn't necessitate enrolling in an ashram or self-imposed seclusion. Sometimes, a few straightforward actions can infuse one's life with mindfulness and positivity.

If you are looking for answers to the questions "What is spiritualism" and "How to develop spirituality," the following methods may interest you? The following ten straightforward measures will effortlessly assist you in adopting a more positive and spiritual lifestyle:

Recognize your concerns: Recognizing your concerns is the initial step toward spiritual development. It could be your behavior, such as anger and restlessness or you could be disturbed by the actions of another individual. It is advisable to enumerate everything that is presently causing you distress.

Determine methods to mitigate problems: The subsequent phase entails evaluating and constructively mitigating circumstances. This implies that you must devise constructive strategies to address the concerns causing you distress. Do you feel agitated or angry?

Try to redirect your attention to an alternative activity. Angered as a result of an individual? Attempt to spend time with considerate individuals.

Collect your thoughts through meditation. Due to our hectic schedules, we often fail to collect our thoughts. Meditation is the most effective method for facilitating this process and enrollment in a class is not even required. Set aside some time, assume a relaxed sitting position and establish a connection with your body with each inhalation.

Develop solid and optimistic convictions: Our convictions are vital to spiritually enhancing our way of life. Our belief system is often the most formidable obstacle to our spiritual advancement. Start by cultivating a positive self-perception, an essential aspect often overlooked, subsequently, advanced towards developing a more expansive and superior belief system.

Connect with others to cultivate your thoughts; humans possess an extraordinary capacity for learning from one another as a species.

Therefore, whether you wish to foster the development of wholesome beliefs or cultivate your thoughts, connecting with like-minded individuals and communities can greatly assist.

Engage in dialogue with a fellow traveler who shares your enthusiasm for spirituality or participates in an online community advocating for this thinking.

Forgive oneself and others; harboring grudges often impedes one's capacity to lead a tranquil existence. We all have fragments of unpleasant past experiences that often reverberate through our minds. You don't have to be with them or their friends anymore, however let it go and move on. (You deserve better)

You must practice forgiveness, whether it involves absolving yourself of wrongdoing or forgiving those wronged you.

Always remember that to progress in life, it is vital to forgive oneself and others.

Develop an optimistic outlook on life and individuals: Cultivating a positive outlook on life and individuals is essential to spiritual maturation. You may fail to recognize its criticality until it is too late.

Every criticism you level at others will provoke negativity within you. Consider the positive aspects of life and the people you encounter; doing so can profoundly affect your existence.

Focus on the essentials and move forward. At some point in our lives, we have all heard the adage, "Move forward on the path of life," but the process is not always straightforward.

Although an approach exists, it is straightforward: prioritize the fundamentals and progressively advance. Create a "To Do" list that includes things you've always desired to accomplish, such as starting a new hobby, changing careers or anything else.

Establishing a schedule is essential, especially if you have a hectic lifestyle and almost no time to devote to learning. It is advisable to conduct a prioritization assessment encompassing professional and personal obligations.

Subsequently, determine the surplus time at your disposal and devise a schedule accordingly. Devote this time to spiritual reading, videos on positive living, meditation and other such activities. A consistent schedule will inevitably accelerate your progress toward your goals.

Discover responses to spiritual inquiries: As one delves further into spirituality, they are prone to confront inquiries that demand clarification. One may acquire spiritual literature on their Kindle and peruse it to discover the solutions to their inquiries. An abundance of spiritual writings exists that can assist you in making strides along this path.

Maintaining a Healthful Lifestyle by Nature.

Adhering to a naturally healthy lifestyle encompasses physical fitness and disease-free status, cultivating a positive mindset, harmonious interpersonal connections, and overall well-being. A healthy person can go from being a couch dweller with aches and pains to having vitality, a sound body and a positive mind.

Listed below are some suggestions for living a naturally happening daily existence.

Performing Exercise

Engaging in physical activity for a mere 15 minutes daily can yield many health benefits, including enhanced joint stability, increased flexibility and range of motion, prevention of osteoporosis and fractures and improved mood accompanied by low symptoms of anxiety and depression.

Exercising doesn't invariably require a gym membership. It can be as straightforward as taking your dog for a walk or turning off the television for an hour while playing outside with your children.

If you are already a regular exerciser, extend your laps in the pool, complete one more set of repetitions or take an additional turn around the block before stopping. Minor increments can have a significant impact.

As forms of physical activity, tasks such as shoveling snow, gardening, raking foliage, vacuuming and sweeping the floor are all included. No one ever stated that exercise must always be vigorous.

Perform jumping exercises or lunges while on the phone and pace during television commercials. Utilize the stairwell rather than the lift or park a short distance from the mall's entrance. Also, dancing is a great option.

Minerals and vitamins

Include in your diet nutrient-dense vitamin and mineral supplements. It has been demonstrated that garlic reduces the risk of many health issues. Herbs, including peppermint, cinnamon and others have been utilized to maintain health and remedy ailments for millennia.

Most food in modern society lacks the vitamins and minerals required to prevent disease. Consider supplementing your diet with vitamins E, D, B-complex and Omega-3 fish oil.

Psychological Health

Emotional well-being is a significant component of a natural, healthful lifestyle. Examine your physique to determine the source of your stress. Maintain a positive social existence by avoiding detrimental situations and individuals. Meditation and relaxation aid in the discharge of negative emotions. For tension reduction, listen to calming music, meditate and take deep breaths.

Further Benefits

Besides fostering a positive emotional state, a wholesome lifestyle offers many advantages. It can aid in the reduction of hypertension, sleep disturbances and the dangers of cardiovascular disease and stroke.

It increases the prognosis for patients diagnosed with head and neck cancer. A diet rich in nutrients and promoting natural health can alleviate the symptoms associated with menopause.

A healthful lifestyle by nature can result in an extended and more fruitful lifespan. You will have the same amount of vitality and experience less pain and disease than you did when you were younger. For many years, homeopathy and other alternative remedies have strengthened and improved the health of your body and mind.

Life is an invaluable bestowment that has been bestowed upon us for a restricted duration. You must, therefore, strive to live a truly remarkable and inspiring existence. Your lifestyle and how you spend your time indicate a great deal about your personality and way of life.

Achieving success in one's life requires years of diligent effort and tremendous self-control. Prominent and accomplished individuals dedicate themselves to these qualities. It is fascinating to discover vital principles that facilitate a successful lifestyle. Take possession of the seven best ones among these:

A thriving lifestyle requires the pursuit of an aspiration or objective. Your ideal ought to be your driving force and you ought to be dedicated to its realization. Many individuals find it extremely challenging to discover their genuine passion. These individuals can simply retain the services of lifestyle counseling specialists to discover their true goals. Each accomplishment in life originates from a goal.

A goal can only become a reality through perseverance and action. Successful outcomes result from being dedicated to one's ideal and enthusiastically pursuing it. The juncture of every virtue is reached through persistence or perseverance.

This particular ability determines success or failure. Your lack of persistence discourages you easily and you tend to abandon your ambitions. Thus, pursuing your goals to achieve the intended results is critical.

To achieve your long-term objective, you must remain open and be receptive to new ideas and suggestions. Coaches of lifestyle choices emphasize the importance of maintaining an open mind and being receptive to new ideas.

Professionals in lifestyle counseling are readily accessible through prominent online marketplaces. These individuals guide cultivating an attitude characterized by gratitude and open-mindedness.

Belief is among the most vital components of existence. In addition to material success, a successful lifestyle also results in spiritual fulfillment. One who believes in divine or preternatural forces is assured of progress in life due to acquiring spiritual knowledge.

This existence is devoid of purpose in the absence of affection. The essence of existence is love. It requires an investment of effort to both love and be loved. Love is one of the most formidable forces that motivates and inspires individuals. In addition, it provides grit when it is required most.

An individual perpetually preoccupied with sensory gratification is less likely to attain a greater degree of happiness and self-actualization than one driven by the intention of serving humanity and behaving as a tribute to society. Positive living and a renewed sense of vitality result from ceasing to be preoccupied with one's interests.

REALIZE YOUR ASPIRATIONS THROUGH POSITIVE THINKING

In the same way that human beings are composed of a bodily structure comprising tendons and ligaments, they also possess a cognitive organ that necessitates the same level of care as the body to preserve optimal health and wellness. The practice of positive thinking can instantly change one's lifestyle.

Our bodies are vital organs that require strict attention and maintenance; if they are negatively impacted, our lives can be drastically and unhappily changed. Those with hypertension must be mindful of their dietary choices, engage in daily physical activity or take lengthy walks to increase their body's vitality and activity. It is not prudent to wait for medical examinations to determine our condition. We must exercise control and initiative.

Our human brain can profoundly change our way of life and our relationships with the world. Suppose one lacks awareness of a negative thought entering their consciousness.

In that case, they will fail to recognize that it will inevitably give rise to additional negative thoughts. Once one focuses on this pessimistic trend, everything appears hopeless, melancholy and hopeless once more, as if one had succumbed to the deception and purchased it.

How often have you observed the pessimistic outlook on life exhibited by others—peers who are perpetually critical of everyone and everything—and, after some time, you realized that you were succumbing to the same behavior?

Unknowingly, negativity can be highly contagious; it is exceedingly simple to become collectively influenced by this unconscious domain. Over time, this detrimental cognitive pattern will have an impact on both one's health and personality.

Life will inevitably become a nightmare if we maintain a pessimistic outlook on the world. Without exception, our expectations will be unfulfilled and everything will appear unfair.

It should come as no surprise that a negative person approaches a problem differently than a positive person; the contrast is night and day. An optimistic individual would confront the issue with assurance, viewing it not as a negative circumstance but rather as a chance to develop personally or professionally.

Also, they acknowledge the potential inability to rectify or resolve the situation; however, this notion would remain at the forefront of their minds and not penetrate their thoughts.

An individual with a pessimistic outlook would perceive this issue as lamentable or perhaps unfixable. Due to their inability to perceive potential outcomes, they would ordinarily withdraw into depression and close their minds.

All of this negativity has a devastating effect on our emotions, lowering the frequency of our energetic vibration to the point where it destroys our immune system, allowing viruses and diseases to penetrate our bodies unprotected. This phrase is not esoteric; it pertains to facts and science you can independently investigate.

Destroying one's existence is unequivocally the only result of harboring negative thoughts.

Changing your thought process will automatically transform your life; while this may initially appear extremely challenging, the formula is straightforward. Positive thoughts can unlock happiness and achievement in one's existence.

Human existence is rife with irritation and tension. Workload, related discomfort and other factors contribute to this phenomenon. One almost forgets to be concerned with their health and those closest to them in the pursuit of financial success and success and rather than being joyful, they become eternally depressed.

One surrounded by vacancy and whose body and mind are ill will appear pitiful. You have no one's attention. At your deepest, most solitary, are you. It sounds abhorrent. But it happens often.

A healthier lifestyle is the most fundamental requirement for an improved existence. By embracing a positive and health-conscious way of life, one can attain joy in one's existence and avert this dire circumstance.

When we hear the word HEALTH, we immediately think of the gym, exercise, a balanced and healthy diet and so forth and individuals typically fear these things. They merely lack the confidence in their abilities to complete these tasks.

Pursuing a healthful lifestyle doesn't entail an excessive amount of effort. Everything begins with your soul's determination. You will undoubtedly succeed in attaining a healthy lifestyle if you possess an unwavering determination to do so. Furthermore, only a balanced diet and regular gym attendance are unnecessary.

Simply incorporating a few straightforward guidelines into your daily regimen will suffice. Maintaining a smile throughout the day, including when you begin, can profoundly impact your life. Yes. Indeed, that is accurate. You will feel more confident and active than ever before. Also, observe that you have not engaged in any physical activity. Such is a healthy way of living.

This is merely the beginning. You can accomplish an increasing amount by implementing a few straightforward guidelines. For instance, for short distances, walk rather than drive. During your morning jogs, keep in mind that you must sweat.

Perform fifteen sit-ups before consuming brunch. Stretch and stand whenever you experience fatigue or lethargy in place of unhealthy snacks, substitute fruit. It is a fallacy to believe that health is improved through gym attendance. That is incorrect. Physical fitness can be achieved through gym attendance but unrestricted hand exercises improve health and stamina.

A healthy body supports a healthy intellect. While an ancient proverb, it remains relevant. A healthy mind and body allow one to attain greater success in life. Always maintains a positive outlook on life. Individuals were greatly impressed by your performance and you will feel tremendously good. You can achieve all of this simply by adopting a healthful lifestyle.

BEN'S MOTIVATIONAL QUOTES

"Fill your future with your dreams. A strong mind leads to big achievements"

Ben Bander

"Don't look back and feel bad. Your future is all about moving forward with hope. "

Ben Bander

"When around people who make you unhappy, remember your own strength. Let go of the heavy stuff and feel light. "

Ben Bander

"If others are jealous, just keep doing well. Let your success show them. Ben Bander"

"Turn every tough time into a chance to get back up. Your mind is your best friend here. "

Ben Bander

"Stay positive even when things are tough. Your peace of mind is very important; keep it safe."

Ben Bander

"Success is all about learning, not losing. Keep learning, and you'll keep moving up."

Ben Bander

"Forget about mistakes you've made. What matters is how high you aim from here."

Ben Bander

"Make your life happy by choosing who's in it wisely. Pick friends who make you feel good and grow."

Ben Bander

"If people are jealous, it shows their issues, not yours. Stay focused on what you're doing, and let your hard work do the talking."

Ben Bander

"Keep moving with hope and big dreams. Every step you take makes worries smaller."

Ben Bander

"Your own hard work lights up your path. Don't let regrets make things dark for you."

Ben Bander

"Leave behind people who make you feel bad. You're strong because you decide, not because others say so."

Ben Bander

"When others are jealous, just keep doing your best. Your success will *speak for itself."*

Ben Bander

"Think about winning and you will. Your mind helps your dreams come true."

Ben Bander

"Welcome change like new friends. The future is a blank page, and you're the artist."

Ben Bander

"Ignore mean words and envy. Your journey is special, and not everyone will get it."

Ben Bander

"When things get tough, be your own cheerleader. Your mind can turn hard times into chances to shine."

Ben Bander

"Stay away from people who mess with your happiness. You need friends who lift you up, not hold you back."

Ben Bander

"Forget about old troubles. Reaching your best self means letting go and focusing on going up, not looking back."

Ben Bander

CONCLUSION

By reading this book, you have learned valuable insights into how positivity can positively change your life. As you finish reading, remember that staying positive is an ongoing journey.

By understanding how thoughts and beliefs work, you have gained important skills to overcome negativity and become more resilient. You have learned that having a positive attitude does not mean ignoring problems. It means facing challenges with a sense of inner strength.

Now you can identify negative thought patterns and break free from self-limiting beliefs. This will help you handle life's ups and downs with flexibility and determination. This book has taught practical tips to nurture positivity, like using affirmations, practicing gratitude, mindfulness and self-compassion.

You have learned how to build and protect a positive outlook.

You can now view setbacks as chances to grow, and celebrate progress towards a hopeful future.

Remember, developing a growth mindset takes time. Staying positive is an ingrained way of life, not a one-time event.

Every day is a chance to renew your outlook. Hardships can become stepping stones if you maintain optimism. Share your positive spirit to uplift others.

I wish you courage to overcome obstacles, wisdom to learn from failure, and confidence to acknowledge your achievements. Using the principles in this book can lead to fulfillment and success.

Your perspective shapes your experiences. Embrace optimism to unlock life's boundless opportunities.

My best wishes for a future filled with happiness, resilience and steady positive thinking!

AUTHOR BIO

Passionate Writer

Ben Bander Abudawood, professionally known as Ben Bander who was born in Saudi Arabia. Ben is a highly accomplished HR consultant, author, and academic with extensive experience in various fields.

My Professional Journey

My professional journey has been nothing short of diverse and exciting. With over 19 years of experience, I've held senior positions in the field of Human Resources in various large companies, particularly in the healthcare and banking industries. As an HR consultant, I've had the privilege of offering valuable insights and guidance to companies across the globe, from the United Kingdom and the United States to the United Arab Emirates and Saudi Arabia.

Academic Pursuits

I believe in the power of education and continuous learning. I hold an MBA degree and a Master's in Organizational Psychology from the United Kingdom. Currently, studying Ph.D. in Organizational Behavior.

Research Interests

My academic journey is fueled by a deep passion for research. I'm particularly interested in employee engagement, recruitment, training and development, gender diversity and equality, organizational behavior, well-being, astrology, and even astronomy. My expertise in these areas allows me to develop effective strategies and interventions to create positive work environments.

Author and Gamer

Beyond my work in the professional realm, I'm also an accomplished author. I've written numerous novels and academic books, covering a wide range of topics, including organizational behavior, leadership, and the intricacies of human resources. Writing is a passion I hold dear.

I'm not just about work, though. I'm also an avid gamer, and I've ventured into the exciting world of game development. I've successfully built and developed several video games, combining my love for gaming with my knowledge of HR and organizational psychology.

Trainer and Lecturer

Education is another aspect of my journey. As a trainer and lecturer, I've had the privilege of sharing my knowledge with over 50,000 professionals in various areas of business management, HR, leadership, interview skills, time management, KPIs, and PMS. My dynamic teaching style has made me a sought-after speaker at conferences and corporate events.

My training extends across the globe. I've conducted sessions in Saudi

Arabia, Dubai, the United States (specifically in Boston and Delaware), UK and the Philippines. It's a gratifying experience to contribute to the growth and development of HR professionals worldwide.

Religious Studies, Theology, and Astronomy

Beyond the professional realm, I have a deep interest in religious studies, theology, and even astronomy. These subjects provide me with a broader understanding of different cultures, belief systems, and the awe-inspiring cosmos.

My commitment to continuous learning knows no bounds.

With my diverse range of skills and experiences, I'm dedicated to making significant contributions to the fields of HR, organizational psychology, writing, gaming, astrology, astronomy, and education. I'm excited to continue this journey, and I'm grateful to have you along for the ride. Feel free to explore my work, ask questions, and get in touch – I'm here to connect and share my passions with the world.

Research Interests

- Employee Engagement: Understanding the intricate relationship with leadership dynamics.
- Gender and Transgender Biases: Analyzing their impact and suggesting potential remedies within HR practices.
- Workplace Well-being: Developing strategies to enhance holistic employee health and job satisfaction.

- Talent Acquisition and Retention: Exploring innovative HR methods to attract, onboard, and retain top-tier talent in competitive environments.

- Diversity and Inclusion: Reviewing HR policies and procedures that nurture an inclusive organizational culture.

- Religious and Theology Studies: Investigating the influence of faith beliefs on society and values and examining the evolution of religious thought in contemporary societal contexts.

Ben is Member in

The Society for Human Resource Management (SHRM).

American Society for Healthcare Human Resources Administration (ASHHRA).

Chartered Institute of Personnel and Development (CIPD)

Copyright © 2024 BenBander

All rights reserved. This work is protected under copyright laws and treaties around the world. No part of this publication may be reproduced, distributed, or transmitted in any form or by any means, without the prior written permission of the copyright holder, except in the case of brief quotations in a review or scholarly journal, or uses permitted by copyright statute that might otherwise be considered an infringement.